I am the Difference

Verses Kindler Publication

Verses Kindler Publication.

Website: www.verseskindlerpublication.com

I am the Difference
By: Mr. Ramesh Kutty Shetty

ISBN: 978-93-49532-53-3

1st Edition

Price: INR 299/$15

Disclaimer

I am the Difference is authored by Ramesh Kutty Shetty. The entirety of this published work comprises the original content of the author, who has undertaken diligent efforts in its editing. The characters depicted herein may be fictitious or inspired by real events; however, they are not intended to cause offense or represent any prejudice against any caste or system. Any similarity to the names of actual individuals, locations, or institutions is purely coincidental and serves the narrative. The author bears sole responsibility for the originality of this work; the publisher assumes no liability thereof.

Index

PREFACE

This is a book that will engage you through my personal experiences in the service industry, which span over the last 30-plus years. I will share simple yet impactful impressions I've had of people—their energy, their emotions, their dedication—and how these elements played a crucial role in delivering superior service.

What makes service truly memorable? Is it the system, the price, the technology, or is it something more human? These are the questions that guided me as I observed, learned, and practiced in the field. Along the way, I realized how much difference it makes when enthusiasm is expressed with balance, when people within a business are respected as its greatest resource, and when teams work together in the spirit of a common goal.

I also came to see that the smallest of signals, be it a warm greeting, a thoughtful gesture, or a consistent impression, can carry the greatest weight in shaping trust. And in an age where change is constant, I have found that certain qualities consistently attract customers, and separate ordinary service from extraordinary experiences. Above all, my journey has convinced me that when emotions are understood and guided with care, they are the strongest asset of any service professional.

This book is dedicated to my dearest mother, my Amma. Her influence has been pivotal, instilling in me the true value of service to humanity.

And it is dedicated to all my readers, who I hope will enjoy this book and immerse in it from the first page to the last. May the stories and reflections here remind you that service is not only about what is delivered, but about the soul, the respect, and the emotion that transforms each interaction into something lasting.

ACKNOWLEDGEMENTS

This book is a piece of my heart, and it would not have been possible without the love, faith, and encouragement of so many people who have stood by me in this journey.

To my Amma, who has always trusted me and my values, and whose love has been my foundation.

To my daughters, Sunakshi (Sona) and Trisha (Chinna), my greatest treasures, my anchors, and my purpose in life. You give meaning to everything I do.

To my sisters, Shashikala (Akka) and Vanita, and my brothers, Prakash (Anna) and Umesh—you, along with my extended family, have been my strength and inspiration, reminding me of where I belong.

To my mentors, the late Mr. Madhu Mangalorkar and the late Mr. Viswam Nair, whose wisdom continues to guide me; to Mr. Bandula Saputhanthiri, whose influence shaped so much of my professional life; and to my dear friend and buddy, Robert Mariaarul, for always walking beside me. I would also like to acknowledge Ravi Nanayakkara his leadership style, which positively impacted my work life journey by fostering a culture of collaboration and helping individuals reach their potential. I extend my heartfelt gratitude to the late Dr. M.S. Rai, a senior aviation medical professional and an inspiring friend and guide. His influence has profoundly shaped my professional journey in India, and I am deeply thankful for his support and mentorship.

To all my colleagues and teammates through the years—thank you for sharing the ups and downs of the journey. A heartfelt thanks to Shruti Kannan and Vikramaditya Mothukuri (Adi), for your trust, support, and friendship at work.

To my friends—Suryakant, Terrence, Bernard, Shubash, Uday, and Dharmesh (Sunny)—your belief in me has meant more than words can express.

And to every single person who allowed me to be a part of their story, you have helped me shape mine.

Above all, I thank the universe for its grace, for guiding me, and for aligning my life with the people and experiences that made this book possible.

Chapter 1: Soul of Service

A Simple Question of Deeper Significance

When was the last time you felt truly served?

Take a moment to think about it. Not when someone arrived with your order on schedule or got a product right, but when you were noticed.

When the person at the counter, behind the desk, or on the receiving end of the phone call made you feel like more than just a task on a list.

It's an oddly tricky question for us to answer on the spur of the moment. We've had thousands of interactions, yes. Effortless check-ins, courteous replies, and fast service.

But how many of them do we remember?

Not for the product. Not for the pace.

But for the way they treated us.

That's what this chapter is about. Not a service as a task. But service as an emotion.

Service is All Around Us—But We Often Miss It

We tend to think of "customer service" in terms of big hotel chains, airline ticket counters, or high-end department stores. But in reality, service resides in the mundane.

It occurs when:

- Your neighbourhood barber knows how you want your hair styled without needing to be told.
- A pharmacist remembers that your mom had a fever recently and asks if she's feeling better.
- A flight attendant offers you a glass of water pre-flight because you appear dehydrated.
- A server at a neighbourhood café addresses you by your name, not merely your order number.
- A hospital receptionist comforts you warmly, even before the doctor appears.

We're always working through these small yet consequential interactions. Some go unnoticed. Others stick with you. Why?

Because service is not merely about having something accomplished, it's about how it's performed.

And more crucially, how it makes us feel in the process.

Systems Work, But Something's Still Missing

These days, we have an app for absolutely everything: QR code menus, self-service checkout lanes, AI-powered chatbots, and automated phone systems. We've never been more efficient.

And something's still not quite right.

You get your food piping hot, your room tidy, your package delivered—but you still leave feeling unimpressed.

Why?

Because systems can fulfil your order, but they cannot fulfil your emotional needs.

They can't provide you with comfort. Or acknowledgement. Or the gentle glow of being understood.

Accurate service isn't about procedure. It's about being there. It's not about box ticking. It's about listening.

A good script and a trained smile can do the trick. However, heart-centred service requires more—it requires an individual who is emotionally present in the moment.

A Story of Two Cafés

I recently went to two cafes on the same day.

The initial one was impressive—clean tables, friendly greetings, and on-time coffee. All the boxes are marked. But the server did not even make eye contact. The establishment functioned like a machine. I paid, nodded, and left.

Later that night, I popped into a smaller café down the street. It was just beginning to drizzle. As I entered, the attendant helped me store my umbrella so that I wouldn't make a mess on the floor. She smiled—not the customer service smile, but the genuine kind.

She said, "Rough day?"

I nodded.

"Let's get you something warm," she said. No upsell, no hurry.

She came back with a note scribbled on the saucer: "Hope this cup turns your day around."

The coffee had the same taste. But the experience? It was as different as chalk and cheese.

One was service. The other was care.

What We Want – The Value of ME

That's the breakthrough in understanding service.

Excellent service is often thought to be about systems, price, or speed. And yes, they are essential. But what we want, and maybe even don't know it, is to feel seen.

That's where the soul is.

My 30+ years of working in the service industry have taught me that excellence is not about luxury; it's about how deeply you can connect with another human being in a time of need.

This chapter delves into that relationship through three core values all customers demand:

- Value for My Time
- Value for My Money
- Value for Me as a Person

Let's start with Time, because in service, valuing someone's time is the initial act of respect.

The Value Triangle

Value for TIME – More Than a Clock Can Measure

Time is the one thing we all want to have more of. So when we surrender it—to wait in line, to call to speak to support, to set up a service—we are placing something valuable in someone else's hands.

In service, time respect is about more than being fast.

It is:

- Holding to commitments.
- Slowing friction.
- Anticipating.

It's not rushing. It's treating the customer with respect, as if their time is essential.

In places where time matters, you sense it in the little things:

- A call that begins on time.
- A doctor who doesn't make you stand around in a hallway.
- A worker who says, "Let me not keep you waiting."

When a customer departs saying, "That was fast and smooth," that's not logistics.

That's service with soul.

When Time Was Respected and It Changed Everything

I recall checking out of a hotel early one morning. I had a close flight to catch and precious little time. The standard checkout routine—billing, bag pickup, and front-desk niceties—would have taken 20 minutes.

The staff had sensed the urgency the night before.

They did it without my request. They organised a wake-up call, pre-checked my bill, had a bellman waiting at the precise moment, and gave me a breakfast box with a note: "Safe journey. We hope your trip is smooth."

The time taken was nothing more than 5-7 minutes and I was able to comfortably catch my flight.

I recall that morning, not because of the breakfast or the ease, but because they valued my time as their own.

Value for MONEY – It's More Than a Price Tag

We tend to think that customers desire the cheapest price. However, what individuals essentially desire is fairness.

We want to feel that what we paid for was:

- Transparent
- Worthwhile
- Not padded with unexpected costs
- Delivered with quality and consideration

Value for money isn't about how much you pay. It's about how much you feel you got in exchange.

I've seen guests happily pay ₹500 for a cup of coffee at a luxury hotel lounge—not because the coffee itself was extraordinary, but because the environment made them feel special. The staff remembered their name, asked about their last visit, and even offered a complimentary cookie with a warm note. The price became secondary to the *feeling* of being valued.

On the other hand, I've witnessed guests complain bitterly about a ₹99 meal deal at a quick-service outlet—because the staff was indifferent, the food was tossed without care, and no one even looked them in the eye. The low price couldn't compensate for the emotional absence.

Value is a perception. It's built not just by numbers, but by gestures, clarity, and respect.

Value for ME – The Heart of Every Experience

This is the hardest value to deliver—and the most rewarding.

Value for ME is about seeing the customer as a human, not a process.

It is about:

- Using their name.
- Remembering past choices.
- Noticing discomfort before they verbalise it.
- Being present in that moment.

This cannot be scripted. It has to be developed through awareness.

When a pharmacist says, "I hope your father is feeling better,"

When the airline staff says, "Would you like to have the window seat again like last time?"

Those are not huge things. But they're the only things the customer will recall.

Because at the end of the day, what every individual desires to know is this: Did you notice me? Did I seem vital to you, even briefly?

That's the soul in service. And without it, all else is noise.

Good vs. Great Service: A Tale of Two Hotels

Let me paint the picture.

Two hotels. Same star rating. Similar architecture. Rooms that cost a few hundred rupees apart.

They both have clean bed linen, okay food, and courteous attendants.

The first hotel follows the book to the letter.

Check-in is efficient. The room is available. The facilities are typical. When I request something, it is delivered within the specified time. The staff smile—but it is the trained smile. All is good. Functional. Predictable.

The second hotel? The check-in begins the same. But as I walk up to the counter, the front-desk clerk greets me with a friendly "Welcome back, Mr. Ramesh." She remembers my request for a peaceful room on a higher floor.

A small, handwritten note lies on the bedside table in my room:

"We hope your meetings go well. We've kept your preferred green tea in the mini bar. All the best."

The difference?

The first made me feel like a guest. The second made me feel like a person.

One was service. The other was connection.

And that's the difference between "good" and "great."

When the System Functions, But the Soul is Absent

I went to a hospital a few years ago to visit a relative who had been brought in for observation. The hospital was state-of-the-art, featuring trendy decor, electronic queuing, automatic billing, and gleaming hallways. The system was impressively streamlined.

Not a single nurse ever made eye contact with the patients.

The executive at the front desk never raised her eyes from the screen.

Physicians moved through the rooms like assembly-line workers, competent but impassive.

The system functioned. No grievances.

But the process was emotionally barren.

It resonated with me on a deep level. For the average patient or their loved ones, it isn't so much about precise diagnostics or a medical summary. It's about reassurance. It's about being heard in a moment of vulnerability.

And that's where this hospital, despite its impressive infrastructure, lost its way.

Because the soul can't be automated.

What Are Touchpoints

In service, we tend to concentrate most on the beginning and the end—how the customer begins the experience and how they depart. However, what creates the memory of service is what happens in between.

These are referred to as touchpoints.

A touchpoint is:

- The initial greeting.
- The tone of an email.
- The pronunciation of your name.
- The instant when you are held up.
- How an error is dealt with.

All of these small things add up to something big: the emotional experience of the customer.

A well-crafted touchpoint isn't perfection. It's more of an intent.

It says to the customer, "You are important at every step."

Miss one, and the entire journey is transactional. But get them right, and even a low-end product feels like luxury.

The Invisible Labour of Emotion

There is a type of work in the service industry that's often overlooked in job descriptions.

It's the emotional labour of:

- Smiling when you're exhausted.
- Listening with care when you're under pressure.
- Calming down an angry customer without taking it personally.
- Being kind, even when the world outside isn't.

This is the invisible work that service staff perform on a daily basis. It's draining. It's rarely acknowledged. And it's critical.

I've witnessed young servers with personal concerns, yet they bring a table to joy with their kindness.

I've seen front-desk personnel negotiate with demanding customers without ever showing anger.

These are not show-stopping moments. But they establish reputations. They are the unglamorous acts that maintain the soul of service.

A Simple Truth

There's a quote I once read that shifted my perspective on service for all eternity: "Service isn't what you do. It's how you make people feel seen."

We're all living busy lives, with heavy days and endless tasks. But in an act of service, when someone takes a moment, looks us in the eye, and sees—that's when something changes.

You're not a booking. A transaction. Or a mere case number.

You're a person.

And that makes all the difference.

The Intangibles That Matter

1. Empathy—The Bridge Between Needs and Response

Empathy is not about having the words.

It's about having the ears.

When a customer comes in upset, confused, or fretful, they may not always use the right words to describe their needs. Empathy enables a service professional to read between the lines, to wait, to be able to say, "It's okay. I hear you."

Empathy is not always spoken. It's in tone, in body language, in pacing.

It's in slowing down when someone's under siege. It's in recalling a face from last week and saying, "How are you today?"

In service, empathy won't fix the issue, but it informs the customer they're not alone in it.

2. Presence—The Rarest Skill in a Distracted World

Being fully present in a service interaction is becoming uncommon.

Too often, we're multitasking—taking an order while glancing at our phones, assisting a guest while thinking about the next task. But presence is what makes a moment real.

I recall a young hotel staff member who assisted me with a late-night issue during my stay. What struck me wasn't his solution—it was how he gave me his complete attention. He wasn't distracted. He wasn't rushing.

In those moments, I wasn't just 'Room 305'. I was a human; heard, acknowledged, and valued.

Presence doesn't necessarily require more time. It just demands more intent.

3. Respect—The Invisible Thread

Respect isn't about saying "sir" or "ma'am."

It's how you communicate, when you communicate, and how you make the other individual feel with the interaction.

It's how you receive feedback, navigate conflict, and respect people's time.

Customers can sense it in an instant—whether they are being listened to or merely endured.

All my years of training teams, I used to say this: Respect is not a strategy. It's a culture.

Where respect goes, so goes trust.

A Story Where Soul Beats Speed and Price

Last year, a colleague of mine was traveling with his mother for her first flight in over a decade. She was nervous, slightly unwell, and overwhelmed by the airport's rush. He had the option to book a free wheelchair service provided by the airline, but he noticed how rushed and mechanical it looked: attendants whisking people from one gate to another like luggage on wheels.

In its place, he opted for a paid premium care service—₹800 extra—but one that assured individualized attention. What ensued made an indelible mark.

As soon as they arrived, a friendly-faced staff member warmly greeted his mother by name. She bent down to her eye level, inquired about how she felt, and spoke to her in her language. They took breaks along the path to the boarding gate so that she might catch her breath. The assistant gave her water and readjusted her shawl when it slipped.

Just before boarding, she said, "This is the first time I'm not afraid of flying."

That one sentence was worth far more than ₹800.

Because what she received wasn't just service—it was dignity, patience, and human connection. No amount of speed or discount can create that.

How We Deliver Time, Money, and ME

Let's get back to the three values that every customer quietly seeks:

Time – Is my time valued, or squandered?

Money – Am I being handled justly?

ME – Do I count as an individual?

When service professionals practice empathy, presence, and respect, these values are delivered naturally. Customers may not express themselves in these exact words; however, they may convey similar sentiments.

They might not mentally dissect it. But they sense it.

And when they do, they return.

Not for the cost. Not for the product. But for the emotion.

The Soul Statement & Final Reflections

The Soul Statement

Let's stop and go back to the heart of this chapter—its core truth: "No machine, no process, no pricing can replace the soul in service."

Systems are crucial. Processes are required. Competitive pricing is sound business.

But none of these, in isolation, can make a customer feel noticed.

None of them can replace the warmth of a genuine smile, the comfort of a listening ear, or the unobtrusive elegance of an individual who extends herself beyond duty.

That instant when a visitor feels remembered. When a patient feels comforted. When a customer feels human, that is what distinguishes a functional experience from a meaningful one.

A Memory That Remained with Me

I want to share the story of two distinct incidents that I was witness to. They both were centered around hotels but the experiences in itself were poles apart.

In one of them, I saw an elderly guest stumble and fall very close to the reception. She was down on the floor, and nobody from the hotel came to her rescue. She must have undoubtedly been in physical pain, but her respect must have been wounded too. And rightfully so.

I rushed to help her, and made her sit up. Then, I raced towards the reception and told them whatever had happened. Although I should not have needed to tell them, because the lady had fallen very close to the reception and they must have surely seen her.

Even after I, another guest, told them about the issue, there was no urgency to take care of the situation. The reception concierge told the bellboy to handle it, and the bell boy told the security person.

And in all this that elderly lady simply sat. She had not received even the basic, humane treatment that all of us are entitled to, leave alone the care that the hotel should have provided her.

In contrast, I saw a heartwarming display of care and compassion being delivered at another hotel.

A man sat alone in the lounge and he had spilled his cup of tea all over his kurta and even on the floor. Before anyone else could move, a young room service personnel came over with a gentle demeanor.

He did not call housekeeping. He did not wait to be told. He just ducked down, gave the gentleman tissues, and said, "Sir, these things happen. Let's get you another one, okay?"

It was five minutes later that the young man came back—not only with a new cup of tea, but also with a folded napkin, a plate of sweets, and a handwritten note that read: "Wishing you a peaceful Diwali, from all of us."

That wasn't training or a scripted performance. It was purely his instinct.

Even from afar, I observed the mood of the guest immediately changing. He smiled, took a sip of his tea, and later at the front desk said, "You have good people here."

That young man's personal touch made all the difference to the guest and his overall experience with the hotel.

When Service Fails to Have Soul

Now, compare that to what happens when there is no soul.

Soul-less service will still get something out to you. It will still get money.

But here's what it won't get:

- Trust – or else, the customer only gets efficiency, not care.
- Loyalty – or else, nothing special was made, nothing memorable.
- Human connection – or else, it never felt like one, helping another—it felt like a task being done.

The harm will not be evident at first.

However, as the gradual decline of repeat business, the absence of referrals, and the slow erosion of brand value become apparent, it becomes clear that customers may not necessarily complain, but they definitely will not return.

And that, in service, is the most significant expense of all.

A Tribute to the Quiet Heroes

Before we close this chapter, I'd like to take a moment to tribute a group of individuals who don't always receive the recognition they deserve: frontline service professionals.

The individuals who:

- Smile even when they're suffering on the inside.
- Soak up frustrations that aren't their own to bear.
- Stand for hours, listen for hours, and care even when no one is looking.

From the airport attendant to the call centre manager, from the cafe waiter to the hospital receptionist—these are the individuals who make the machine of the service economy run smoothly.

Their labour can be intangible on balance sheets.

But it is remembered in the hearts of all who have ever known they were cared for, in the least expected ways.

To them, I dedicate this chapter.

Because they are the soul in service.

Closing Reflection

And so we finish this chapter. Here is one last thing I want to leave with you: "Soulful service is not a luxury. It is the only kind that lasts."

Products will change. Technologies will shift. Expectations will increase.

But the need for humans to be noticed, valued, and cared about—that will not change. Never.

So, the next time you're serving a customer, keep this in mind:

They might not remember your badge, your pitch, or your script.

But they will always remember how you treated them.

Chapter 2: Energy with Enthusiasm

Introduction: The Energy Behind the Experience

Every service experience begins with a feeling.

The expression of service is what forms the first and most lasting impression in the mind of the customer. Sometimes this expression is verbal, shaped by the words we use. And sometimes it is physical, which gets conveyed through gestures, tone, and body language. But very often, it is completely intangible. It cannot be seen or heard. It can, however, be strongly sensed through the energy that someone brings into a space.

At the heart of every memorable service moment lies human expression. At the heart of every expression is one crucial force: enthusiasm with energy.

No matter how perfect the systems may be, how incredible the product is, or how polished the environment looks- these things are not what create the real impression of a service. That's created by the people.

The enthusiasm they bring becomes a direct extension of the service itself. The way they show up, respond, engage, and serve all is a clear indicator of the kind of enthusiasm and energy they are bringing.

And this plays a crucial role in changing the overall experience of a customer.

Let us understand this better through an example.

A middle-aged lady goes to a diagnostic centre for some tests. The atmosphere is all silent and rather scary, and hence, the patient is naturally a little tense.

Now imagine two possible scenarios.

In the first, the receptionist at the counter greets her with loud cheerfulness. "Good morning, ma'am! How are you? Here for your health package, right? Don't worry, it'll all be smooth!" The receptionist talked fast, quickly handed over a bunch of forms, and started explaining everything in an animated tone.

She did everything else that she was required to, except for one thing. She failed to notice how overwhelmed her customer looked.

Although the receptionist was trying to be friendly, her energy only heightened the patient's nervousness and anxiety. The tone didn't match the mood. The customer didn't feel cared for, but instead she felt rushed, perhaps even a little dismissed.

In the second scenario, the receptionist makes gentle eye contact, smiles softly, and says, "Good morning, ma'am. Welcome. You're here for the check-up, correct? Let me help you with the form. Please take a seat if you'd like."

She speaks in a calm voice, keeps the conversation brief but kind, and allows the woman to settle into the moment.

There was no exaggerated energy and no over-enthusiasm in her interaction. There was just a display of understanding and warmth, but from a respectable distance.

Here, the patient feels acknowledged. She may still be anxious, but she senses that the establishment respects her pace.

This is a true service impression; not just based on efficiency or decorum, but on the emotional tone created through the person delivering the experience.

This is where the language of service lives. It is not comprised just of words, but of how those words are spoken, how actions are delivered, and how the customer feels while receiving them.

Now let's take a closer look at what we call the people aspect of service.

In any setting, a person involved in service can play one of three roles:

1. Directly delivering the impression – such as a receptionist, technician, front-office executive, nurse, or sales assistant who has firsthand interactions with the customer
2. Supporting the impression – such as a coordinator, scheduler, kitchen team member, or backend administrator
3. Leading the impression – such as a manager, supervisor, or team leader guiding the service experience

Each of these roles has a different point of contact with the customer.

But in each, the way enthusiasm and energy are expressed makes a significant difference.

Let's say someone is delivering the impression directly. Their voice, posture, attentiveness, and even facial expressions are in full view of the customer. Their energy must be alert and warm, yet not overpowering. If they're too cheerful in a tense moment or too dull in a celebratory one, the emotional mismatch creates discomfort.

On the other hand, someone supporting the delivery of impression may not interact with the customer, but their energy shows through the service outcome—how timely a room is cleaned, how well the equipment is arranged, or how smooth the process feels. Their enthusiasm lies in their discipline and detail, and its impact is no less than that of a frontliner.

Finally, a leader sets the tone for the entire team. Their enthusiasm must be both inward and outward. They should uplift their team without overwhelming them, and guide the environment in a way that channels energy responsibly. Their role is not just to be positive, but to help others balance their energy and adapt to each situation with emotional maturity.

What remains common across all these roles is the need for balance.

Whether you are interacting with the customer, supporting those who do, or leading the people who shape the experience, the enthusiasm you carry must be thoughtful.

Not exaggerated. Not missing. Just tuned.

This chapter explores that tuning.

It shows how energy in service is not about being loud or lively—it is about being emotionally intelligent. It is about presence. About knowing how to read the moment, how to respond in proportion, and how to create comfort not just through actions, but through how those actions are expressed.

Because in service, what truly lasts is not performance. It's presence.

And that begins with understanding the soul of enthusiasm, which is characterized by being caring, confident, and always considerate.

Service without Stillness: A Personal Story

There was an incident that truly got me thinking about the role that a service professional has in making or breaking the overall experience for a customer.

And the foundation of playing that role properly lies in being able to be enthusiastic and energetic, but in the right measure.

I had visited a familiar restaurant which I had previously visited in the recent past. It was one of those days where I was looking forward to a quiet dinner with myself. Not necessarily silence, but certainly some space. Some personal time.

As I entered, I noticed a familiar face among the service staff. He noticed me too. And before I could even make my way to the host stand, he approached me with a beaming smile. He greeted me warmly, addressed me by name, and welcomed me back in a way that felt both genuine and enthusiastic. He remembered everything, right from the table I preferred to the one dish I typically order.

At that moment, I felt seen and valued. His energy was unmistakably positive, and his attention to detail was impressive.

It felt good; like I truly mattered in that space.

He personally escorted me to my table, pulled the chair for me, and ensured I was comfortably settled in. I appreciated the gesture. After all, we all like to be remembered, don't we? That initial interaction set the tone for what I thought would be a great evening.

But then, something changed.

As the evening progressed, I noticed that he was around me a little too often. He came over to check if the starter was alright, not once but twice. Then he returned again to ask if I wanted anything else. Then, five minutes later, he came by with a napkin I hadn't asked for, followed by a casual check-in about how my day had been. He smiled, he hovered, he stayed just long enough to break the rhythm of my evening.

Now, let me be honest. I admired his enthusiasm. His intent was pure, and I could tell he genuinely wanted to make my experience wonderful.

But over time, his presence felt less like thoughtful service and more like constant surveillance. I had come back expecting the same care, yes, but also expecting space.

At some point, I had to gently say, "Thank you, I'm good for now. I'll call you if I need anything."

I didn't want to offend him or dampen his spirit, but I had to express to him what I truly needed.

Reflecting on that evening, I realized something important about service.

In that experience, everything else was great, right from the food, to the ambiance. But one thing tilted the balance: the inability of the service professional to sense when enough was enough.

His energy and enthusiasm, which initially made me feel appreciated, eventually overwhelmed me.

It wasn't about what he said or did; it was about how often, and how persistently he did and said things.

As a customer, I never stopped valuing his intent. But there was a mismatch between what I needed and what he offered.

He didn't notice that I had begun leaning away slightly when he approached, or that my responses had shortened. These were subtle cues that I wished he had picked up on.

This, to me, is the heart of the conversation around balance in service energy.

Service is not just about starting strong. It's equally about knowing when to pause, when to step back, and when to simply hold space.

Enthusiasm without observation can quickly turn from delight to discomfort. Energy, if not adjusted to the moment, becomes noise.

As a service professional—whether you're delivering the service, supporting it, or leading it—you need to be fully present, fully energized, and fully available. But not always visible. Not always engaging.

Because true service is not about constantly proving your presence. It is about offering it when needed, and withdrawing it when it's not.

This balance is not easy to strike, but it's essential.

And let me clarify something important here: It's not merely about turning the energy down.

In fact, my experience in the restaurant would have been worse if the server was dull and indifferent. It's all about channeling it appropriately.

You can be fully charged and still composed. You can be passionate without being overpowering.

That evening taught me that a service impression is not only shaped by what you offer, but by how and when you offer it. And unless the person serving understands that rhythm, even the best intentions can fall out of tune.

When Enthusiasm Is Not Balanced

Service, at its core, is about energy exchange.

Every time a customer walks into a service environment—be it a store, hotel, clinic, salon, or even a helpline—they enter with an emotional expectation. Sometimes it's joy, sometimes urgency, sometimes quiet detachment.

In that moment, the energy brought in by the service professional acts as a mirror. The emotional outcome of the interaction is entirely dependent on how well that energy is matched,

Enthusiasm, in this context, is a beautiful thing. It communicates warmth, interest, presence, and commitment. When it's well-timed and authentic, it can transform an ordinary moment into something memorable.

But when it is not balanced it starts to distort the experience rather than enhance it.

And this applies for both an excess of enthusiasm as well as a lack of it.

Let's explore how this imbalance plays out.

Imagine a spa. The air is scented with lavender, the music is soft, and a guest walks in after a long week hoping for silence and relaxation.

But the moment she enters, the receptionist springs into a rehearsed monologue. She is bubbly, loud, and starts hurriedly offering packages, introducing product combos, cracking jokes to seem friendly, speaking a bit louder than the environment calls for. She means well. She's eager to please.

But her energy is out of sync with the space the guest is trying to enter, both mentally and emotionally. This guest didn't come for attention or bubbliness. She came for peace.

What was intended as helpfulness now feels intrusive.

Or picture a fitness club where a trainer, full of positive intent, keeps interrupting your routine with high-fives, pep talks, and energy bursts, even when you're trying to focus on your exercises.

You may appreciate their spirit, but after a point, it starts to feel overwhelming. You feel watched. You feel like you have to perform, rather than simply exist.

This is what happens when enthusiasm isn't modulated.

The customer feels obligated to engage, even when they didn't ask for that level of interaction.

The focus shifts from the customer's comfort to the service person's energy.

And on the other side of the spectrum is lack of presence. Opposite in its effect, but equally damaging.

You walk into a premium retail store. The lights are perfect, the music ambient, the display well-curated. But the staff barely glance your way.

There's no smile, no welcome, no eye contact. They're not rude, but they are not there for you. They end up coming across as silent, mechanical, and perhaps unbothered. You walk around, unsure if they're available, wondering whether your presence matters at all.

It's not bad service in terms of process, because you will still be able to buy the products that you came for.
But it lacks life. It lacks warmth.

This is the absence of energy and enthusiasm about what the customer is there for. And just like too much enthusiasm can make a customer feel smothered, too little makes them feel unseen.

Even worse, it makes them feel like the brand doesn't care.

And that is a far more dangerous impression than a delayed delivery or a technical mistake.

The emotional impact of this imbalance is often quiet, but lasting.

- A customer overwhelmed by loud, over-eager service may smile politely but will never return.
- A customer made to feel invisible may complete the transaction but will tell others that the experience was cold.
- A customer who expected calm but received performance may feel emotionally drained, even if the service was efficient.

In both cases, there's no "incident" to complain about. No fight, no argument, or no broken policy.

But something still feels off. And that feeling is powerful enough to undo every other effort made by the brand.

Because customers don't leave because of one mistake.
They leave because of how they were made to feel.

Here's what's important to understand: the customer doesn't separate the person from the brand.

When a guest interacts with a single staff member—be it a front desk executive, a cleaner, a nurse, or a salesperson—their behavior becomes the face of the entire brand at that moment.

- If the person is warm and responsive, the customer says, "This brand gets it."
- If the person is overbearing or indifferent, the customer says, "This brand doesn't care."

Impressions are built in seconds, but they linger for much longer.

And when the service energy is misaligned, what remains in the customer's memory is not the décor, the pricing, or even the product.

It's the emotional mismatch. The dissonance between what they felt and what they needed.

Every moment of customer interaction becomes a building block of the brand. And when the energy shown by staff is not in tune with the customer's emotional state, it begins to wear down trust, slowly, silently, and often invisibly.

Here's how:

- Loss of loyalty: The customer might not complain but they won't return.
- No word-of-mouth: People only recommend experiences that feel emotionally right.
- Eroding brand tone: If too many service touchpoints feel inconsistent, the brand starts losing its emotional identity.
- Staff disconnection: Employees who are not trained in emotional calibration either become over-performers (who burn out) or disengaged (who fade into the background).

Why Balance Is Not Optional; It's Essential

The truth is simple: Too much energy is not professionalism. Too little energy is not humility.

Balance is not a compromise, rather a critical skill.
And it must be taught, practiced, and valued at every level of service delivery.

Great service professionals know this.

They don't just walk into an interaction. They walk into a customer's emotional landscape, and they adjust their energy like a thermostat: warmer when needed, cooler when required, and always present in just the right amount.

That's the difference between serving with routine and serving with presence.

Tools to Maintain the Balance

Balancing enthusiasm and energy in service is not about being less of who you are. It's about becoming more attuned to the other person. It's about recognizing that service is not performance but presence.

In this section, we explore the five essential tools that help service professionals regulate their energy.

These tools are not just helpful, but they are necessary for meaningful human connection. Each one allows a professional to gauge, adjust, and express their presence in a way that suits every customer's unique requirement.

1. Anticipation vs. Assumption: Don't Just Know—Observe

One of the most common mistakes in service is assuming too quickly.

We often jump to conclusions about what the customer wants, based on our previous experiences or standard procedures. But assumption is a shortcut. It skips the part where we pay attention.

Anticipation, on the other hand, is a skill. It's the ability to quietly read a situation and offer what the customer needs, sometimes even before they ask for it.

Instead of a service professional directly thinking, "This customer looks like they're in a rush, let me skip the formalities," pause for a moment. Look for cues in their body language, tone, urgency in speech. Maybe they're just a little distracted, not in a hurry.

A helpful way to avoid assumptions is to gently ask, "Would you prefer a quick overview, or shall I walk you through everything?" This keeps the power in the hands of the customer.

Assumption rushes to impress but anticipation waits to understand what is truly required.

2. Emotional Intelligence: Sense Before You Serve

Emotional intelligence isn't about being emotional, but about being emotionally aware.

It's the ability to detect what someone might be feeling, even if they don't say it outright. And in service, this ability transforms how you show up.

Before stepping into an interaction, take a moment to notice the emotional tone of the person in front of you. Are they cheerful, tense, distracted, calm, or reserved? Their voice, eyes, posture, and choice of words will give it away.

For example, if someone answers your questions in brief sentences and avoids direct eye contact, perhaps they aren't in the mood for detailed conversation. Respect that space. Let your energy match theirs, and not overwhelm it.

Without emotional intelligence, enthusiasm can become noise. With it, energy becomes empathy.

And empathy is remembered far longer than efficiency.

3. Empathic Listening: Don't Just Hear—Feel

Most service professionals are taught to be "good listeners," but empathic listening is something deeper.

It's not about waiting for your turn to speak and instead, it's about letting the customer feel heard without interruption or judgment.

If a customer says, "I'm just so frustrated, nothing seems to be working today," the instinct might be to offer a solution immediately. But empathic listening means pausing, validating, and letting them feel acknowledged first.

You could respond with, "That sounds really exhausting. Let's see how I can help you feel a little lighter right now."

It's in that thoughtful gap between their concern and your action that the real connection is built.

Empathic listening softens the environment. It builds trust. It reminds the customer that they're not just being processed, they're being cared for.

4. Social Awareness: Match the Space, Not Just the Person

While emotional intelligence is about reading one-person, social awareness is about reading the environment and adjusting your presence to match it.

Every space has its own energy—a bustling call center, a quiet hospital waiting room, a crowded check-in desk, or a solo customer in a quiet store.

You may be someone who naturally speaks with animation, gestures broadly, and smiles a lot. But if you're serving in a room where others are silent and tense it's important to soften your tone and presence to match the space.

Being aware of the collective energy of a space helps you avoid jarring the environment, even unintentionally.

Great service professionals don't just connect with individuals; they also blend into spaces. They know how to shift gears without losing authenticity.

5. Situational Awareness: Let the Moment Guide You

Sometimes, balance isn't about what the customer says or shows. It's about what the situation demands. This is where situational awareness comes into play.

It's the ability to understand the larger context and adapt your approach accordingly.

Let's say you're a delivery executive and it's raining heavily. You reach the doorstep soaked, and the customer is annoyed by the delay. Situational awareness helps you resist the urge to explain or argue.

Instead, you acknowledge the inconvenience, and calmly offer the parcel with a respectful, "Sorry for the wait—I appreciate your patience."

In another case, if you're a manager supervising a long queue, instead of continuing regular service, you step in, communicate updates clearly, reassure people, and regulate the energy in the room. You're not reacting, but you're responding to the moment with awareness.

Situational awareness makes your presence relevant. It transforms enthusiasm into *timely presence*. And that creates an impression of care and professionalism—even in chaos.

Bringing It All Together: Two Different Customers, Two Balanced Experiences

Let's imagine two completely different customers. Both deserve good service—but what that means for each of them is very different.

Customer A: The Reserved Introvert

- Enters a retail outlet quietly, avoids eye contact, looks around calmly.
- Doesn't pick up any product, just browses.

Balanced Response Using All Tools:

- The staff doesn't jump in with offers (anticipation), but stays observant.
- They read the quiet mood and approach gently (emotional intelligence).
- When they ask, "Would you prefer to browse freely or shall I walk you through?"—they're practicing empathic listening.
- Their tone is soft, they keep physical distance, and avoid hovering (social awareness).

- They notice the customer leave without purchase and simply offer a soft, "Hope to see you again," rather than trying to close the sale (situational awareness).

The customer walks away not feeling pressured, but respected.

They may not buy today, but they will remember how they were treated.

Customer B: The Curious Conversationalist

- Walks into a wellness clinic for the first time.
- Asks questions about the treatments, chats about her week, and smiles often.

Balanced Response Using All Tools:

- The staff picks up the openness and engages with warm, active energy (anticipation).
- They respond with appropriate excitement and information, without oversharing (emotional intelligence).
- They let the customer talk and shape the direction of the conversation (empathic listening).
- They create a comfortable zone for dialogue, ensuring they're not distracting others nearby (social awareness).
- They offer brochures, pause for questions, and pace the interaction according to her mood (situational awareness).

The customer feels seen, heard, and supported—and forms an instant connection with the brand.

Implementing these tools is not difficult. But they require awareness.

And awareness requires slowing down; not just physically, but even mentally and emotionally.

Whether you're greeting someone at the reception, offering help at a billing counter, guiding them through a consultation, or delivering a product to their door, your energy leaves an impression.

And when you use the right tools—observe instead of assume, sense before you act, listen without preparing a reply, adapt to the space, and honor the situation—your service no longer feels like a routine. It feels like care.

How to Implement This Balance

Balancing enthusiasm and energy in service isn't about suppressing who you are, but about refining how you express it.

While awareness helps you understand the need for balance, it is the daily practice of certain habits that allows you to apply that understanding with consistency and grace.

1. Tone Modulation

Tone is not just the sound of your voice; it's the emotion you carry in your words.

And tone modulation does not just mean speaking softly or loudly; it's about tuning your tone to the mood of the moment.

A service professional must learn to read subtle emotional cues and adjust their vocal energy accordingly. A cheerful greeting may uplift one person, but may come across as tone-deaf to another who's visibly tired or anxious.

Knowing when to keep your tone bright, when to mellow it, and when to let silence speak is a practice that deepens over time and with self-awareness.

2. The Power of a Pause

In service, speed is often mistaken for efficiency. But in human interactions, the most powerful tool is the pause. A brief moment of silence before responding, suggesting, or solving.

That pause gives you time to process, time to observe, and, most importantly, time to respond rather than react.

It creates room for the customer to express themselves more clearly, and for you to offer support that is timely and relevant.

3. Micro-Mirroring

Closely linked to modulation is the skill of micro-mirroring, where your body language, tone, and pace subtly reflect the customer's natural rhythm.

If someone is speaking slowly, processing carefully, and seems reserved, meeting them at that same rhythm fosters trust. If they are animated and expressive, matching their energy can help you build rapport.

Mirroring gently signals alignment, helping customers feel safe and understood without a single word about it.

4. Boundary Sensitivity

One of the hardest skills in service is knowing when to exit gracefully. Many well-meaning professionals linger too long in the name of warmth or attentiveness.

But attention, when prolonged, can become surveillance.

Many service professionals mistake presence for persistence. They linger longer than needed, check in too often, or hover in an attempt to be helpful.

But often, the most valuable service is the space you give a customer to breathe, reflect, and engage on their own terms. After you've provided the necessary guidance or assistance, knowing how to withdraw while still remaining accessible is a mark of maturity in service.

5. Internal Energy Check

Every professional carries emotional residue from the previous interaction.

Without realizing it, we may walk into a new conversation holding the stress, irritation, or momentum of the last one.

Taking a moment to reset and asking yourself, "What state am I in?" or "What does this next person need from me?" can completely shift the tone of the service you deliver.

It creates a clean emotional slate and ensures that each customer receives your presence, not your leftover reactions.

These tools, when practiced regularly, become habits. And habits become instincts. Together, they form the invisible foundation of a well-balanced service experience—one that is enthusiastic, but not intrusive; warm, but not overwhelming; present, but never performative.

They allow service professionals to calibrate their energy moment by moment, person by person, because the best service is never generic. It is tailored, respectful, and alive to the human in front of you.

At its heart, balanced enthusiasm is not about doing more or less. It's about doing what's right for the moment.

When service professionals learn to adjust their tone, pause with intention, read emotional cues, respect space, and reset their own energy, they stop merely serving and start connecting.

These are quiet tools but they lead to powerful impressions. Because in the end, what customers remember isn't how energetic you were.

It's how thoughtfully you showed up for them.

Chapter 3: Respecting the Resource

Revealing the Most Important Resource

What is the most valuable resource in a service business?

Is it the product—the item that is carefully prepared, branded, and sold?

Is it the ambience—the warm lighting, the curated playlists, the comfortable seating, and small knick knacks kept to appease customers?

Is it the systems and processes—courteous greetings, ease and convenience, and an experience of being treated like royalty?

These elements undoubtedly matter.

But are they enough to truly create a connection and set a business apart?

Let's consider an example.

A restaurant has impeccable food, a pleasing atmosphere, and ticks all the boxes of a luxury experience.

As its popularity spread, a chef from a rival restaurant sampled some of their best-selling dishes and was able to recreate them. The décor, cutlery, and ambience were replicated. And all the tangible elements of the first restaurant are easily adopted by its rival.

Yet, the business continues to thrive.

There is something that keeps customers coming back to it; something that the rival cannot copy.

Moving away from theoretical examples, I invite you to think back to your most memorable service experience.

Was it strictly because of the product you purchased or the environment you experienced? Unlikely.

What you remember and what truly stayed with you was a person.

A person who smiled at you without needing to.
A person who anticipated a need before you voiced it.
A person who made you feel seen; not as a customer, but as a human being.

In every service business, the most important resource is not what you build, but who you build it with.

The most important resource is the people.

They are the brand, the culture, the tone, the warmth, and the experience; all rolled into one living, breathing presence. You can automate systems. You can outsource operations. You can redesign the physical space.

But what you cannot replicate, automate, or mass-produce is the effect of a person who genuinely cares about the experience they are creating for someone else.

It is the people who carry the heart of your service. And if you want to improve the service, you must first invest in them.

What Does this Resource Need?

Nurturing this powerful resource does not need anything extraordinary. It needs something very simple, and foundational.

All it takes is respect.

Respect is what breathes life into performance. When people feel respected, they show up differently. There's a quiet confidence in their tone, a natural warmth in their engagement, and a sincerity in how they handle challenges.

Respect isn't just a moral principle; it's an energy. It shows in how someone stands, speaks, listens, and responds.

Respect tells a service professional, "You truly matter to what we are building here."

It tells them that they contribute much more to the business than the mere tasks that they complete. It conveys that they aren't just there to fill a role, but to make a difference.

And that message, once internalized, becomes the starting point for every great customer experience.

When respect becomes a part of the culture, it creates an environment where people uplift one another. They collaborate better. They support more. They don't just do their job, but perform in it with all their heart and soul.

This is the foundation. Everything else in service, like tone, technique, systems, or policies can be taught. But what makes people shine from within is the feeling that who they are, and what they bring, is seen, valued, and honoured.

Respect doesn't need grand speeches or bold declarations. It lives in the small and everyday actions of how feedback is given, suggestions are welcomed, or contributions are acknowledged.

And when the most important resource in a service business is respected, it gives back in the most remarkable way. Not just with better work, but with deeper care.

A Personal Experience: The USP of a Coffee Shop

I am a frequent visitor to a renowned coffee shop. It has all the requisites to be a big success; a popular and central location, a warm and cozy interior, consistently good coffee, and great food too.

Over the years, it's become my go-to space for catching up on work, spending good times with family and friends, or simply unwinding.

But something struck me during one of my recent visits.

I started wondering: Why have I kept coming back here for so many years? Is it just the ambience? The coffee? The decor? It's not like there aren't other cafés around, some even trendier, newer, or more spacious. And yet, this place held its grip on me—and many others like me—year after year.

So that day, I decided to observe my experience more deliberately.

The first thing that stood out was the doorman. He didn't just open the door mechanically, like he was a doorman doing his job. He greeted guests with a warmth that felt personal, like someone welcoming you into his own home. His nod wasn't hurried. His smile wasn't rehearsed. There was something host-like in the way he held the door. It was evident that this place and the people walking into it truly mattered to him.

Inside, the barista didn't just take orders. He acknowledged regular customers by name, remembered preferences, and even knew who liked their coffee in a take-away cup even when they were sitting in.

The servers worked in a way that again felt deeply personal and yet was extremely efficient. They didn't hover, but were always aware.

You could see them picking up on cues; clearing a table just when someone started gathering their things, bringing water before someone asked, offering a warm napkin on a rainy day.

It wasn't service for the sake of doing it. It was service with a sense of care.

That day, I stayed longer than usual.

As the lunch crowd thinned and the place quieted, I noticed a man I'd seen several times before. Like usual, he gave me a warm smile and then went about his day. He wore no name tag, no particular uniform, and yet he was everywhere.

I saw him wipe the mirrors and the basin outside the restroom, restock tissue boxes, and discreetly switch off the fans in the shaded corner of the café where no customers were seated anymore.

None of it seemed rushed or imposed. There was a calm attentiveness in the way he moved; like he cared about the space and did everything not because he had to, but because it mattered to him.

Curious, I approached him and struck up a conversation. I asked him how long he'd worked here and how he managed to carry out so many different tasks, always with such ease and positivity.

He smiled and without taking a second, he immediately answered, "I do everything from my heart because I love this space. And I love this space because I feel respected here."

That answer stayed with me.

He went on to tell me how the owner knows him personally by name, checks in on his family, and has invested time and money to train him in coffee preparation and food handling.

"He says I should know everything in the café, so I can grow. That's why I give my best. Because I'm not just working for this place. I'm working with it."

That simple distinction—not for, but with—hit me with clarity.

When someone begins to work with a business instead of just for it, everything changes.

It's no longer just about tasks and responsibilities. It becomes about ownership. There's a difference between a person who shows up to complete a job, and someone who shows up to contribute to something they feel proud of.

And to enable a person to transition from the former to the latter, all that's needed is respect.

When people feel respected in their workplace, something unlocks inside them. They start caring about things beyond their job description. They notice details others miss. They step in before they are asked. They offer suggestions not to prove a point, but because they genuinely want to make things better. They see the business's success as their own. That's when they stop functioning as employees and start behaving like partners.

At that moment, the entire experience of the café made sense to me.

It wasn't just about the coffee or the lighting or the menu. It was about the people. And more importantly, what those people felt. They felt respected and seen. And because they felt respected, they offered a kind of service that no training manual can enforce and no process can replicate. They offered presence, pride, and personal investment.

That man at the coffee shop wasn't paid extra to restock tissues or to make sure the fans weren't running wastefully. No one told him to check the restroom mirror or offer help when the barista was short-handed.

He did it because the environment had nurtured a sense of belonging in him. Because when people feel respected, they feel responsible not by force but by choice.

And this is where businesses often experience the real, tangible benefits of this intangible culture.

A team that feels respected performs more consistently. They handle complaints with composure, because their self-worth isn't under attack. They collaborate more smoothly, because they don't feel the need to compete for recognition. They adapt faster, stay longer, and speak more positively about their workplace even outside of it.

The ripple effect is enormous.

Customers feel the difference, even if they can't name it. They feel it in the warmth of service, in the attentiveness of staff, in the invisible care woven through the entire experience. And when customers consistently feel seen, respected, and valued, they come back. Not just for the product, but for the people.

This is what builds loyalty and recognition for a particular brand.

The business starts to be known and recognized by its people, and that identity becomes its strongest asset.

How Respect Transforms People and the Business

Respect is the invisible ingredient that transforms a workplace into a place of belonging. It turns employees into ambassadors, tasks into gestures, and service into care.

And for a customer, it makes the difference between merely visiting a place of business and feeling like a valued guest in someone's space.

1. It Leads to Emotional Investment

Respect makes people feel important. This feeling of importance, in turn, leads to them caring deeply. Not just about their tasks, but about the entire experience they help deliver and how the business flourishes.

They begin to pay attention to the small things not just related to the customers but to the overall health and wellbeing of the business.

This is not just the mechanical fulfillment of duties, but are gestures rooted in emotional presence. They happen when a staff member doesn't just do their job, but becomes personally invested in how it's received.

And this kind of commitment rarely comes from orders or checklists. It comes from feeling respected at work.

2. It Perpetuates a Positive Cycle

There is a direct and powerful link between how people are treated within an organization and how they treat those outside of it. When employees are treated with patience, kindness, and trust, they naturally pass that forward.

This forms a positive cycle; a Loop of Respect of sorts.

Respect, when given to employees, does not stay hidden. It travels with them to the reception desk, the checkout counter, the call centre, the housekeeping floor. It reflects in their tone, their willingness to listen, their attention to detail, and even their body language.

The inverse is also true. Disrespect, when internalized, leaks out in the form of coldness, sarcasm, disengagement, or indifference toward guests. That's why customer satisfaction is often a reflection not of strategy, but of culture.

3. It Encourages Stability and Retention

Employees who feel disrespected rarely stay, and even if they do, they tend to emotionally withdraw. But those who feel respected often stay through the ups and downs not because they're tied by a contract, but because they feel valued.

Respect builds stability. It reduces friction, lowers absenteeism, and builds a foundation of trust. A consistent team creates a consistent experience for customers. You don't have to constantly retrain or rehire when you respect the people you already have.

That's another special aspect I even noticed about the coffee shop. Over the span of almost 7 years that I have been visiting it, almost all the faces remained the same.

In a day and age where people are quick to switch jobs, the fact that this place had managed to retain most of its staff for so long was a clear indicator of how well they were being treated.

Stability also breeds loyalty. Not just toward the brand, but toward the team. People show up for one another, cover for each other, and share knowledge more freely when they feel they are part of something that values them.

4. It Sparks Initiative and Ownership

Perhaps the most underrated gift of respect is that it gives people the confidence to own their role.

When people feel respected, they stop waiting to be told what to do. They start noticing what needs to be done and also do it. They act with initiative. They respond to situations instead of reacting. They propose ideas, solve problems, and take responsibility without being chased.

For instance, a respected concierge may step out of their desk to personally assist a lost guest. A respected cashier may quietly notice that an elderly customer needs help with a heavy bag.

These small moments of initiative add up. Over time, they define the difference between a business that merely functions and one that flourishes.

5. It Strengthens Brand Identity from Within

A respected workforce doesn't just perform better; rather, it represents better. They become walking, talking extensions of the brand. Their energy, attitude, and behavior become the most honest advertisement of the company's values.

When service professionals feel respected, they hold themselves to higher standards. Not because they're afraid of punishment but because they take pride in the uniform, the badge, the name tag.

They begin to carry the brand not just on their clothes, but in their conduct.

And in the world of service, this lived brand is often more powerful than any marketing campaign.

Respect is often misunderstood as a soft, sentimental ideal. But in the world of service, it is a strategic imperative.

It creates loyalty, stability, initiative, brand consistency, and emotional richness. It strengthens every interaction, be it between colleagues or with customers. And most importantly, it turns a workplace into a place of purpose.

The Ways in Which Respect Can Be Shown

Respect, when practiced intentionally, becomes the soul of a service business. It's not a single act, but a consistent pattern in how people are treated day after day, task after task.

Let's explore the many ways in which respect can be tangibly and practically shown in a service environment.

1. Through Growth Opportunities

One of the most meaningful ways to show someone they are valued is to invest in their growth.

Growth here doesn't always mean climbing the hierarchy or adding fancy titles. It means giving people the opportunity to learn, to evolve, and to develop new abilities that increase their sense of self-worth.

When you tell someone, "I believe you can do more than you're doing right now," you're not just helping them grow. Essentially, you're respecting who they are and who they could become.

It shifts the person's perception of their job. They no longer feel stuck in a repetitive task and instead see themselves as an evolving contributor.

In a mid-sized salon, a hair assistant who mostly swept floors and washed tools showed a quiet curiosity about haircutting.

Instead of dismissing this as "out of scope," the salon owner began assigning her to observe stylists, attend product demos, and eventually assist with simple hair styling on quieter days.

A year later, she was one of the busiest junior stylists, with regular clients asking for her by name. Her transformation didn't begin with a promotion. It began with someone saying, "You have potential."

That act of respect rewrote her future and boosted the business with one more skilled, passionate professional.

2. Through Autonomy

Autonomy means allowing people the freedom to make small decisions in their area of work.

It is the opposite of micromanagement. Autonomy sends a simple but powerful message: We trust your judgment.

When service professionals are given the space to think, act, and improvise, they feel a sense of responsibility. They begin to think not just about "doing what I'm told," but "doing what's best for the situation." That sense of empowerment breeds pride, creativity, and a deeper emotional connection to the business.

A steward in a hotel banquet hall noticed that guests often struggled to find water stations during large conferences. On his own, he began placing small glass jugs on the center of each table during breaks. This wasn't part of his assigned duties, but it made the experience smoother for attendees.

When the banquet manager learned about it, she didn't reprimand him for "going off script." She thanked him, praised the initiative in the daily briefing, and told the team that such thoughtful autonomy was welcomed.

From then on, the team felt encouraged to think beyond rules. Their mentality shifted from being mere employees to instead being hosts. That shift, powered by respect, elevated the overall service culture.

3. Through Recognition

Recognition is the art of truly seeing people. It's not limited to awards or employee-of-the-month banners. It lies in daily affirmations, spontaneous praise, and quiet acknowledgment of effort.

It means noticing the details others miss: who cleaned the counter when no one asked, who helped calm a frustrated guest, who stayed back to fix a small error without complaint.

When people feel recognized, they feel humanized. They're reminded that their work matters, their presence is noticed, and their efforts are not invisible.

A senior patient care coordinator in a diagnostic clinic made it a point to thank the front desk team at the end of every rush hour. Just a small sentence like, “You all handled that morning queue so calmly today,” did the trick.

Over time, this simple habit made a visible difference. The team’s posture changed. There was more laughter. More mutual help. And fewer complaints of burnout. They felt acknowledged not just when things went wrong but when they quietly did things right.

Recognition didn’t cost the business anything. But it earned emotional loyalty.

4. Through Emotional Safety

Respect also means creating a space where people feel safe to speak, question, and be themselves.

Emotional safety is a culture where no one feels mocked, humiliated, or silenced for making a mistake or asking for help. It is the foundation of psychological well-being in any workplace.

In service environments where pressure and urgency are constant, emotional safety ensures that staff don’t internalize stress in unhealthy ways. It builds teams that are more resilient, collaborative, and stable.

A service technician at a luxury car dealership accidentally installed a wrong accessory and only realized it the next morning. Nervous, he confessed to his team lead.

Instead of reacting with blame or punishment, the lead asked, "What did we learn?" and then guided him to rectify the situation.

The technician, relieved and grateful, later said he worked with more confidence because he no longer feared being 'caught'. That confidence translated into more consistent service delivery and a longer retention with the business.

5. Through Rituals of Care

Culture is not built by policies. It's built by rituals. Small, consistent habits that communicate care and connection form the emotional rhythm of a workplace.

These rituals could be simple: checking in with each team member during a shift, celebrating small wins, remembering birthdays, or allowing a few minutes of team debrief after a difficult customer interaction.

Such rituals remind people they are not machines. They are individuals in a shared space, and their emotional presence is valid and valued.

In a boutique clothing store, the team gathered every morning for a 5-minute "circle talk"—a quick round where everyone shared one thing they were proud of from the previous day. This tiny routine began to build emotional closeness. Team members began helping each other more, solving problems together, and laughing more with customers.

One junior member once said, "This morning talk makes me feel like I matter before I start working." That's the impact of care woven into routine; it becomes respect lived daily.

6. Through Inclusion in Decision-Making

People feel respected when they're not just expected to follow rules, but are invited to shape them. Involving frontline staff in small decisions about workflows, uniforms, layout, or even menu changes can be a powerful sign of trust.

When people are asked for their opinion, they feel heard. And when their opinion is used, they feel valued.

A mid-range hotel was redesigning the welcome drink menu and casually asked front desk executives what most guests had been enjoying or asking for lately.

Their input shaped the final list and their pride was visible when guests complimented the changes. One of them said, "I feel like a contributor, not just a receptionist." That shift in mindset came from being included.

7. Through Consistency

One underrated but essential form of respect is consistency. Treating people fairly, applying rules evenly, and maintaining clear communication builds a foundation of emotional safety. Inconsistent leadership—where praise, criticism, or rewards feel random—can create insecurity and resentment.

Consistency tells people, "You won't be surprised or blindsided here. We'll treat you the same way today as we did yesterday."

In a medical reception team, one employee was often praised while others felt overlooked. Over time, performance declined and team morale dropped. The team lead then began maintaining a weekly rotation of appreciation, thanking one member for a specific contribution in front of the group. With this, the entire team's engagement visibly improved.

Respect isn't just about spotlighting one star. It's about building a consistent sense of fairness that lets everyone feel seen.

Respect vs. Incentive

Understanding the difference between these two terms is what makes all the difference in a business.

One of the most common and often well-meaning misunderstandings in service businesses is the confusion between respecting a resource and incentivizing a resource.

It isn't always a careless mistake. In fact, many business owners and managers genuinely believe that giving bonuses, commissions, or financial perks is the highest way to show that they value their people.

The logic appears simple: if someone performs well, you reward them monetarily. Isn't that a sign of appreciation?

To an extent, yes. Fair compensation, periodic financial recognition, and performance-based rewards are certainly an important part of how an employee feels valued.

But respect, in the truest sense that this chapter has explored, is something deeper.

It is not tied to performance outcomes or targets alone. It is rooted in how a person is treated as a human being, regardless of the numbers they produce.

And that makes all the difference.

The confusion arises because incentives are visible and quantifiable. They can be charted, measured, and budgeted.

Respect, on the other hand, is more subtle. It is not always easy to measure, and it doesn't show immediate returns on a profit-and-loss statement. But it shows up powerfully in the long-term culture of a team.

Let's understand this with a theoretical lens before we move to a real-world example.

- Incentive is a transaction. It says, "If you do X, you will receive Y." It is goal-oriented and externally driven. It focuses on behavior that aligns with the company's performance metrics.
- Respect is a recognition. It says, "I see you as a person, not just a role. Your effort, presence, and identity matter, even when there's nothing to count or celebrate externally." It is relational, intrinsic, and not tied to any conditional result.

The real difference is in the intention behind the gesture and the emotional response it creates in the person receiving it.

Incentives can bring joy, but they don't always bring belonging. Respect, on the other hand, can bring commitment, pride, and a sense of personal stake, even without the promise of a financial reward.

Let's look at a real example to see how this difference plays out in practice.

Example: Two Teams, Two Cultures

Imagine two teams working in two different hotels. Both hotels are similar in size, location, and service offerings. But their internal culture is built on very different principles.

In the first hotel, every employee knows there is a performance-linked bonus system. If a staff member receives above-average ratings from customers, or completes a certain number of hours without complaint, they are eligible for monetary rewards.

On the surface, this seems motivating. And in the short term, it is. Employees work fast, try to hit benchmarks, and smile through shifts. But over time, cracks begin to show.

Staff begin to compete for recognition. Small conflicts arise over who served which table or which floor. When a team member is going through a hard time and underperforms, others silently distance themselves, because collective targets may suffer.

The emotional climate is sharp, calculated, and somewhat tense. The language is results-first. People are working to earn their due, not because they feel truly connected to the work or to each other.

Now consider the second hotel.

Here too, there are performance assessments and occasional rewards but the real culture is built around respect. Every team member is greeted by name when they walk in. Their ideas are listened to in team meetings, even if they are junior. They're encouraged to take pride in their role, and mistakes are treated as moments of learning, not judgment.

When someone performs exceptionally well, they are not just rewarded. They are publicly appreciated for the way they made someone feel, not just for what they did.

One day, a guest left a handwritten note at the reception thanking a housekeeper named Reema for her quiet kindness during their stay. At the next team huddle, her manager read out the note aloud and then turned to her. Not with a gift card, but with a simple statement: "Reema, the way you show up every day reminds us why our work matters."

Reema beamed. She felt something no bonus could give her—a sense of dignity, meaning, and belonging.

This is the difference.

In the first hotel, incentives created effort but the mindset remained external. In the second, respect created ownership. People didn't just show up to do their jobs. They showed up to care.

When Respect and Incentive Work Together

At a bustling city-based customer care center, the days were long and emotionally draining. Agents had to handle dozens of calls every day; many of them from anxious or irate customers facing issues with internet or power outages.

There was a performance bonus in place. Those who resolved the most calls in a day, with minimal callbacks, were awarded a monthly bonus. It worked, to an extent. The numbers were met.

But what made the center truly successful wasn't just the incentive program.

The management took time to create a culture of respect. Each employee was given a voice; there were biweekly team meetings where feedback wasn't just gathered, but acted upon.

Managers made it a point to check in not just on work targets but on how their people were doing. Struggling team members were mentored, not scolded. Quiet wins were celebrated. Training wasn't limited to technical skills and it even included modules on emotional resilience, listening, and even self-care.

One team leader noticed that a particularly quiet employee who rarely hit targets had a knack for handling difficult, upset customers. Rather than replace him, she had a conversation and shifted his focus to escalated cases. He thrived. And the respect he felt made him double his commitment to the role.

This is what happens when people are respected as human beings and not just measured as data points. The incentive gave direction. But the respect gave them identity.

Their mindset shifted from "I have to do this to get my bonus," to "I want to do this well because I matter, and so does my team."

They felt part of something. They owned their roles. And they showed up with more care, not just more efficiency.

When Incentive Is Offered Without Respect

In contrast, consider a popular fashion retail chain that prided itself on aggressive sales. Every salesperson had a clear incentive structure, and higher sales meant higher commissions. The message was simple: sell more, earn more.

On paper, it seemed effective. Sales were steady, and top performers were rewarded publicly. But below the surface, cracks had begun to appear.

New staff were rarely trained beyond product knowledge. There was little to no team bonding. Management interaction was strictly about targets. No one asked employees about their comfort, their aspirations, or their struggles. Everything boiled down to how much they sold.

It started showing. Staff members began hoarding customers. When a new client walked in, two or three employees would subtly compete for their attention. Arguments broke out.

When someone had a bad week, they were mocked, not mentored. The pressure to perform was immense, and turnover became a monthly routine. Staff weren't loyal; they were tired, disconnected, and replaceable in their own eyes.

I spoke to one of the salespeople there once. She said, "We're only as good as our last bill. No one really knows who we are here. We're just numbers on a sheet."

This is what happens when a business tries to substitute respect with reward. Incentives may get you performance, but without the glue of dignity and trust, that performance stays fragile and unstable.

In the long run, incentives without respect often lead to burnout, toxicity, and transactional behavior. Employees start saying, "This is not my problem," or "Let me just finish my part and go." The sense of collective ownership is lost.

The Shift in Mindset

So, what's really different between the two workplaces?

In the first, people felt seen. They felt like they belonged. That made them want to protect the brand, grow with it, and give their best, even on the tough days.

In the second, people felt used. They performed, yes. But always with a watchful eye on what they'd get out of it. There was no bond. Only transactions.

And this is the heart of the matter.

- Incentive creates action.
- Respect creates commitment.

You need both. But never confuse one for the other.

Respect doesn't cost a business anything extra. But it gives back in the form of loyalty, consistency, initiative, and emotional investment. It is the silent foundation on which great service is built. Without it, even the best incentives can't stop a team from falling apart.

Conclusion

In the world of service, there will always be rivals who do the same things as your business, or perhaps do things even better.

But the one thing no competitor can replicate is your people and the way they make others feel. And that magic doesn't come from manuals or metrics. It comes from a deep, unwavering sense of being respected.

When individuals are treated with dignity—not just hired, but heard; not just tasked, but trusted—they begin to show up differently. They stop working for the business and start working with it. That shift from compliance to commitment is what creates unforgettable service.

So if you're looking to build a brand that lasts, don't just invest in strategies or offerings. Invest in the people who bring them to life. Because when you nurture the soul behind the service, the business doesn't just grow.

It flourishes.

Chapter 4: V (We) is the Rule of the Game

V is for Victory And for 'We'

In the last chapter, we reflected on a simple truth—people are the most important resource in any service business. When even a single person is treated with respect and given a sense of belonging, they have the potential to transform how a customer perceives a brand. This eventually determines the overall success of the business.

But if one person can have that kind of impact, imagine what can happen when these numerous powerful resources come together.

Here's a simple example to understand this better: Can any of your fingers, individually, eat, work, or do any of the things that your whole hand does? No! These actions can only happen when each finger contributes and does its part. No one finger is as effective as the fist that forms when they all come together.

That's the power of a team. A team unified not just by job roles, but by a shared sense of purpose. That is where true excellence in service is born.

Because in service, there is no "I" that can win alone. It can only happen when every individual is in sync, and they all come together with the same sense of responsibility and shared pride. That is the true force multiplier of service.

Service is not like a solo sport. It's not about who works the fastest or who smiles the widest. It's more like a symphony, where different instruments play at different times and in different ways, but all working towards one melody.

The cleaner who resets the space before the next guest arrives, the back-end scheduler who ensures appointments are smooth, the customer care agent who resolves an issue gently, the barista who hands over the coffee with warmth—all these acts together form a single customer experience.

One touchpoint may stand out, but the magic is always in the collective rhythm.

Think about any seamless service experience you've had. Be it at a salon, restaurant, shopping mall, or even a simple coffee shop.

Was your experience just one person's doing? Absolutely not.

It happened because every individual played their part with a shared mindset, which was to serve you well. If we zero in on the example of a salon, every person involved there was doing different things. The hair stylist cut your hair up to your expectations, the sweeper ensured you walked into a clean space, another staff member offered you beverages, someone was making sure the music and lighting created a pleasing atmosphere, and the watchman outside ensured your vehicle was parked safely.

The tasks were different, but they were all towards the same goal. They made you feel valued as a customer and served you well. That is the essence of "We."

It is the realization that every person involved in the business is a part of a team, and every goal is a part of that team's shared goal.

It happens when every person is committed to their own duty, but they are also working towards a much larger goal that goes above and beyond their own duty. That's the essence of a team mentality.

Working like this entails coordination, collaboration, and communication.

Think of these as the three pillars of the 'We' mentality because till these are not in place, that team cannot really be formed.

Coordination is when different roles are aligned like moving parts of a well-oiled machine. Imagine a hotel where a guest checks in early. The front desk doesn't just smile and say "your room will be ready at 2." Instead, they discreetly check with housekeeping, who signals that a room is already prepped and clean. The luggage team is looped in immediately, and within minutes, the guest is settled into the room; all because people anticipated the sequence and moved together. That's coordination in action. It is silent, seamless, and satisfying.

Collaboration is when different departments or individuals step beyond their own silos to support a bigger goal. Consider a dental clinic where a receptionist notices a nervous patient in the waiting area. Instead of just calling the patient when the time comes, she informs the assistant to spend a few moments casually talking to ease the tension. The dentist, upon being told, adjusts the pace and tone of their conversation too. Each person did a little more than their technical role not because they had to, but because they chose to work together in the interest of comfort and care.

Communication is the bridge that keeps everyone aligned and informed. Think of an airline where there's been a gate change or a flight delay. The ground staff updates not just the announcement board, but also informs the café inside the lounge so they can hold off on clearing out guests too quickly. They notify the cleaning crew so they can prepare the new gate ahead of time. Everyone knows what's happening and can act accordingly.

That's how communication prevents confusion and protects the customer experience from falling through the cracks.

A front desk may check you in. But if the room isn't ready, the whole impression breaks. A call centre executive may take your complaint, but if the technician doesn't show up, the promise fails. And yet, when teams work with the mindset of "us," these fractures disappear.

Everyone begins to operate not in isolation, but as part of a larger, living organism. The kind where every small gesture builds toward a shared outcome.

This shared ownership also transforms how outcomes are received. When a customer leaves happy, it's not about giving credit to one department. It's about recognizing how everyone came together to make it possible.

On the flip side, if something goes wrong, the goal isn't to assign blame but to solve it together and brainstorm how everyone can contribute to avoiding it in the future. That's what builds emotional safety within teams and trust within the brand.

And this isn't just theory. I have seen this principle be reflected in the culture of every truly successful service brand.

Be it a luxurious resort, a bustling store, a small café, or a hospital ward; if customers are returning, remembering, and recommending, there's almost always one invisible reason: *The people there think and operate like a team.*

They don't just deliver services. They deliver impressions, together.

Because every service interaction, no matter how brief, is a performance that requires multiple artists behind the scenes and on stage. And when all of them move in sync, with the same goal in mind, that's when the experience turns from satisfactory to unforgettable.

So this chapter is not just about teamwork. It is about collective intention.

It's about adopting the mindset that in service, Victory ('V') only happens when there is 'We'.

A Blockbuster Experience

Let me pose a question here- Why do you go to movie theatres? My reasons include things like seeking entertainment, relaxation, and a brief escape from other thoughts or responsibilities. I'm certain that most of you go for similar reasons.

So, one part of the total experience rests on the movie itself. Because if it fails to entertain you, the main point is lost. That, however, is not something that the movie theatre itself can control. It is controlled by yet another team (including actors, directors, musicians, costume and set designers, storywriters etc. who must work together to make the movie worth-watching). But that's a discussion for another time!

Right now, I invite you to think deeper about the other part of your total experience.

It rests on the service environment of the theatre.

It is not determined by the responsibility of one individual or one department; rather, it is the cumulative result of many people doing their work with care, awareness, and a shared mindset.

We walk into the theatre expecting a calm, inviting environment. Is the entry area clean and comfortable? Is the lighting welcoming? Does the space make you feel like you've stepped into something special?

And if all these boxes are ticked, you are a satisfied customer.

Every person who helped to create and maintain that space is responsible for this outcome. Right from the person keeping the floors clean to the person replacing the fresh flowers there; they are each adding up to your experience.

You, as a guest, may never actively notice that the restrooms are spotless or that tissues are refilled, unless something goes wrong. But these behind-the-scenes roles are essential. A baby changing station being hygienic and stocked, accessible pathways for differently-abled guests, clear signboards put up to show people where they have to go- all these are service essentials and a result of team work.

Now, imagine that you are expecting a few more people arriving for the film, but they are running late. You are probably stressed and anxious about missing the film. The person in-charge at the ticket counter will offer to hold the remaining tickets, while the usher will help your friends find their seat. Both professionals work hand in hand because they are both tuned into the same goal: keep the guest experience stress-free.

In the same manner, the ushers and other staff who guide guests to their respective screens, or ensure that aged guests or young children are escorted safely even in times of massive rush are working with other people to provide comfort and care to the highest possible degree.

Then comes the turn of the people working at the various counters in the theatre premises. Enjoying popcorn and other snacks, or sitting for the movie with a glass of a chilled cold drink is equally important for the guests, because it is a part of the relaxation they are coming for. A guest who misses the opening scene due to delays at the food court will carry that frustration throughout the show.

But efficiency isn't about just rushing, because that may lead to compromised food quality or messed up orders; thereby again displeasing the customer. What it needs is impeccable coordination behind the scenes. The chefs, the server, the billing executive; all need to work in rhythm. One delays the chain, and the whole flow breaks.

When the food arrives hot, the order is accurate, and the counter staff says, "Enjoy your movie!"—that's a team functioning as one.

The theatre screen, audio, and air conditioning are something that we rarely think about. Because they are almost always in perfect condition, and we never stop to think about the work that goes into keeping it perfect and the people who take it up. Yet, their contributions are crucial. A blurry screen, a distorted speaker, or a freezing cold hall can shatter the mood, no matter how good the film.

The technicians, light controllers, and equipment handlers often operate in isolation, far from the customer's view. But like the rest of their team, they are focussed on only one outcome and perform it diligently in the way that they can.

What makes this possible?

Knowing that their work directly impacts what the guest feels, even without being seen.

Their silent commitment to excellence despite not being client-facing is the backbone of the experience. And when they align their intent with the rest of the team—to create immersion, not just function—it shows.

When all these individuals work with the mindset that their job is not just their job, but part of something larger and something meaningful, the result is a cohesive, delightful experience. The theatre doesn't promise the quality of the movie, but it can promise the quality of how the guest feels during it.

That's the difference between staff who are trained and teams who are aligned.

Because in the world of service, victory (V) is not achieved through "me"—it is built through "We." When every greeting, every cleaned surface, every warm gesture, every quiet act behind the scenes comes from a place of collective ownership, the guest doesn't just remember the movie. They remember how they felt.

And that's the mark of a truly great service culture.

Hospitality in Harmony

I had checked into a hotel with friends and family during a festive long weekend. As expected, the place was packed with guests. We smoothly completed the check-in formalities and a porter was arranged to take our luggage up to the room. I was a happy customer. But once we actually got into the room, that changed quickly.

I observed that the bed had extremely evident stains on it, and hair strands were distinctly visible on the linen. I immediately called and asked to speak to the manager. She looked respectful and attentive the whole time and politely told me, "Sir, I apologize for the inconvenience you have faced. This is not how we want you to start your stay. We will do everything possible to make sure the problem is solved. Sadly, all our other rooms have been booked out so I cannot offer you a replacement, but please allow me some time to see what can be done."

Within the next 5-10 minutes, there was a knock on my door. He assessed the entire problem, apologized yet again, and then said, "Sir, I will definitely change the linen and other bedding. But if you will allow me, I would prefer to change the mattress too for you to ensure that you face no other problems with the bed."

I was impressed with his customer-centricity and the fact that he was willing to go a step beyond to rectify the issue. However, I was concerned about the time it would take to arrange for a new mattress, have it brought up to the room, and then have it changed.

When I expressed this to him, he said with a smile, "I have a fresh mattress waiting right outside the room. And it will not take more than 20 minutes to get it all changed."

I was left even more impressed. Anticipating the need of the customer, the young man had already coordinated with the concerned people and had come equipped with everything that would be required.

As he began his work, he was joined seconds later by two more staff members. They worked in synchronization, like the cogs of a single machine.

A few minutes later, there was a soft knock on the door and a server walked in with a large tray. The entire mechanism of the hotel had been spurred into action and I saw the teamwork that must have gone into this gesture. The pantry, the barista and baker, the servers had all been galvanised. Complimentary cappuccinos and freshly baked cookies were sent to the room to ensure that we were comfortable during the time that your room was ready.

The manager, true to her word, finished the other work that she had to cater to and personally came up to the room to check on the progress. Being in the service industry for so long, I have become very good at reading even the subtlest of gestures shown by people. I could see that she was definitely happy about the resolution, but she was also surprised. Especially when she saw the new mattress and the refreshments tray.

I could not hold myself back from asking her about what had astonished her.

She gave me a smile, gestured towards the young man who had handled my problem so well, and said, "Sir, I'm surprised because I hadn't got the chance to tell him the problem in detail. I merely told him that this room's bed was not clean. I was surprised at how he thought about getting a replacement mattress or even this refreshment tray."

Hearing that the young man wasn't even aware of the full problem, my curiosity piqued even further about how he had prepared so perfectly to address my issue.

When I asked him about it, he simply said, "Sir, it didn't matter whether I knew all the details. I knew everything that I needed to know- that there was a cleaning issue with the bed. I didn't want to come here and then start running around for a solution, so we all coordinated to ensure an extra mattress was already delivered here.

As for the coffee and cookies, my colleague estimated that the cleaning would take a bit of time, however efficiently we tried to do it. She took it ahead to the concerned people and they came up with this resolution."

Hearing this, it was now my turn to be surprised.

What unfolded there was a beautiful synchrony of roles and responsibilities.

It showed me that this was more than a team that followed orders. It was a team that functioned like a family- watching out for and supporting each other, helping without being told, and most importantly, caring about what a guest might feel.

Various people came together and worked in harmony. And this was not because they were specifically directed to do so, but because they saw it as their shared responsibility.

It wasn't just the problem-solving that impressed me. It was the orchestration; the unspoken rhythm of service that happens only when everyone is aligned to the same purpose.

In hindsight, the issue with the bed has faded in memory. What has stayed with me is the way it was handled. Not by one person, but by a team that moved as one.

That night, I didn't just experience service. I experienced culture. The kind that says: "No matter what our role is, we are all responsible for the impression we leave."

And that, to me, is the essence of true service victory.

A victory earned by 'we,' not 'me.'

The “I” Mindset: Dedicated, But Disconnected

Let us try to understand the basic difference in mentality in both these approaches to service. Through the example of a restaurant, we will uncover what happens when people work with both these distinct mindsets.

In the “I” version of the evening, every person shows up with a clear understanding of their own task and sticks to it.

It is not ‘wrong’ in the strict sense of the word. But it definitely does not achieve the wonderful outcomes that come with a ‘We’ version.

The valet opens car doors, hands over the token, and moves on swiftly. He doesn’t bother checking if a guest looks lost or unsure. After all, helping with directions isn’t in his job role.

The hostess checks the reservation list and directs the guest to the designated table. She doesn’t notice that the guest is carrying a baby stroller and is being led to a spot with tight spacing. “That’s for the server to manage,” she tells herself.

The server walks over promptly, delivers menus, and takes orders with precision. He is quick, polite, and efficient. But he doesn’t observe that the guests are struggling to hear each other because the air conditioning vent is blasting cold air directly over their table. He shrugs it off, because facilities issues are not his domain.

The manager, meanwhile, is at the front attending to an incoming VIP booking. He’s not monitoring the floor or the real-time experience of current guests because the operational flow seems fine on paper. Every task is fulfilled, every person efficient, every part in motion.

Yet, for the guests, something feels lacking.

They aren't neglected. But they aren't truly cared for either. The interactions feel mechanical. The transitions are clunky. No one is rude, but no one seems to own their experience either.

It's a collection of people doing their jobs, but it doesn't feel like a team serving them. There's no invisible thread tying it all together. The restaurant functions but it doesn't connect.

The "We" Mindset: A Cohesive, Living Organism

Now picture the same restaurant, the same time of evening, but with a different energy. An energy powered by a shared goal: Make the guest experience seamless and joyful.

The valet welcomes guests warmly, noticing that the elderly woman stepping out of the car is wearing heels and might need a steady arm. He offers it naturally and communicates her arrival discreetly to the front desk through his walkie.

The hostess, having received that message, immediately alters her seating plan to assign the guest a table with easy access and a cushioned chair. She walks over with a smile and briefs the server in charge — "Table 4 has an elderly guest, let's make sure the room temperature is comfortable."

The server greets the table warmly and, before handing over the menu, gently offers to adjust the AC vent near the table. He notices that the family seems unfamiliar with the cuisine and offers to bring out a couple of tasting spoons for their top-selling dish. He steps into the kitchen and shares the guest's preferences directly with the chef.

In the kitchen, the chef doesn't treat it as an extra burden. He appreciates the heads-up and instructs his line cook to prepare two small portions for sampling. The food runner waits an extra minute to ensure those samples are plated nicely; a small detail that makes a big impression.

The manager, instead of waiting at the front, walks the floor periodically — not to monitor, but to support. When he hears that a guest is celebrating a birthday, he doesn't just approve a complimentary dessert. He checks in with the barista to prepare a customized note with the dessert plate, and cues the staff to time its arrival for when the cake is being cut.

In the back of the house, the person in charge of cleaning dishes, who rarely sees guests, hears about a sudden shortage of side plates and steps in to ensure fresh ones are ready. He moves beyond the pile of dirty dishes to refill the server's shelf; not because it's his job, but because he knows it helps the team.

The entire team is coordinating, collaborating, and communicating. Every action, every micro-decision is tied to a bigger purpose of not just "doing my job," but "making our guests feel valued."

The Difference in Energy

The contrast is subtle in some places, and striking in others. But the difference in mindset is unmistakable.

In the "I" mindset, each person is dedicated. But they view the restaurant as a series of departments, not as a single body. They focus on efficiency. But their view is narrow, and bound by their task lists and roles. Success is completing what they were assigned.

In the "We" mindset, each person sees themselves as part of a living, breathing organism. The team feels like one body, where the eye informs the brain, the brain instructs the hand, and the hand supports the leg. Everyone's role matters and they still do their respective duties very well.

But more importantly, everyone knows they are working toward *one* shared outcome of delivering an outstanding experience.

Success isn't just "I did my job." Success is "We worked together to achieve what we all want to."

This difference changes everything.

It's what makes a restaurant memorable instead of just functional. It's what makes a guest return; not just for the food or decor, but for the warmth, the ease, the feeling of being truly taken care of.

And most importantly, it's what transforms a collection of employees into a *team.*

How to Instil and Cultivate the 'We' Mindset

Building a team mentality doesn't happen by accident. It has to be consciously seeded, nurtured, and embedded into everyday operations.

A shared purpose is not something you declare. It's something people come to believe in, because they see it being practiced all around them.

Elaborated below are some ways to help cultivate this mindset in any service-oriented team, with each approach grounded in real, collective examples that show how great service is not about individuals excelling in silos, but about many hands shaping a unified experience.

1. Onboarding That Speaks of 'Us', Not 'You'

The mindset of new team members is shaped from the very first day. If onboarding focuses only on personal responsibilities, people begin seeing themselves as isolated cogs in a machine. But when onboarding emphasizes interdependence, shared outcomes, and team identity, new hires immediately understand that their work contributes to a greater purpose.

For instance, in a boutique hotel, new joiners spend their first week shadowing multiple departments—front desk, housekeeping, kitchen, even the technical team. They're not being trained to do all the jobs but to understand how each role contributes to the guest's experience.

One day, a new front desk associate watched the engineering staff fix a room's faulty lighting just before a VIP check-in, while the housekeeping team coordinated to adjust turn-down service timing.

Witnessing such seamless interdependence early on sets the tone: no task is isolated. Every action connects to a larger promise.

2. Shared Language and Internal Phrases

Language is culture. The words a team uses can reinforce the spirit of teamwork or fragment it.

A shared vocabulary—unique terms, internal phrases, team mantras—can create a sense of belonging and reinforce that everyone is rowing in the same direction.

At a family-run restaurant chain, staff use the term "table memory" to refer to sharing guest preferences internally across teams. If a server notices a child prefers their pasta without sauce, that becomes "table memory" for next time. The host, the kitchen, and even the person clearing the table are informed during daily briefings.

It's not about who gets credit. It's about making the family feel remembered, no matter who serves them.

3. Shadowing Beyond Job Roles

True team understanding doesn't come from job descriptions. It comes from seeing how others work and how their work fits into the bigger picture. Shadowing across roles builds empathy, patience, and a deeper respect for how the service chain functions.

In a large multiplex cinema, new food court team members spend a day watching the ticketing staff manage long queues during peak hours. Then, they rotate to the usher team, understanding how show delays affect snack purchases. This holistic view makes everyone more flexible and understanding.

On a particularly packed Saturday, a ticket agent voluntarily helps in the food counter to manage rush, while an usher keeps guests informed to ease frustration.

Everyone knows the system only works when people step in beyond their lane.

4. Cross-Functional Training for Fluid Support

Flexibility is the heartbeat of a strong team. Training team members to offer basic support in other functions means that service never crumbles under pressure. This creates a culture where helping each other isn't seen as extra, but rather is expected.

In a busy café, baristas are trained not only in coffee preparation, but also in basic table service. During weekend brunch, when waitstaff is overloaded, the baristas help refill water, clear empty cups, and even take quick orders.

In one instance, a customer spilled their drink. While a staff member from the floor ran to get napkins, a barista paused his brewing task to help clean up, and the manager walked over to offer a fresh drink.

This quick, collective response diffused the situation instantly. The customer wasn't helped by one efficient employee, but rather they were cared for by a synchronized team.

5. Visible Team Rituals that Reinforce Unity

Rituals are powerful reminders of what a team stands for. They create predictability, build connection, and ensure that even in the busiest moments, the team pauses to align. When rituals include everyone and highlight interdependence, they naturally strengthen the 'we' bond.

Every evening in a fine-dining restaurant, there's a five-minute "sync circle" before service begins. Each department—chefs, stewards, hosts, and servers—shares anticipated rush points or special guests.

Recently, during a VIP birthday dinner, the pastry chef shared the surprise dessert sequence with the whole team. The host greeted the family warmly, the servers built anticipation, and the lights and music were timed just right; all because of a ritual that aligned their intentions.

The result? A seamless, magical experience that no one person could've created alone.

6. Peer Recognition in the Moment

Recognition isn't only a leader's job. When peers regularly acknowledge each other's effort, it nurtures mutual respect and reinforces the idea that everyone is watching out for one another. It makes teamwork visible and celebrated.

In a premium spa, a team message board is used to post "quiet shoutouts." When a towel staffer helps front-desk staff during a rush by prepping guest kits, or when a therapist quickly re-adjusts schedule gaps to accommodate a delayed guest, peers acknowledge it on the board.

These small acts of recognition create a culture where people look out for each other not for rewards, but because they feel valued by one another. Team pride grows stronger when teammates are each other's biggest supporters.

7. Leadership That Models 'We' Every Day

Culture follows leadership. If leaders operate in silos, teams will too. But when leaders show up side by side with their teams—especially during high-stress situations—they communicate the strongest message: "We are in this together."

In a resort during the monsoon season, unexpected power issues created chaos. The GM didn't stay in the back office. She stepped out, helped reassure guests, stood with technicians inspecting the switchboards, and even coordinated umbrellas for waiting arrivals. Inspired by her visibility, the heads of housekeeping and kitchen coordinated logistics like flashlight distribution and contingency food supplies.

Her actions showed that leadership isn't about directing from afar; it's about showing up and standing with the team. That day, the guests praised not just the quick fix, but the visible unity of the staff under pressure.

Conclusion: The Power of Many, Moving as One

In the world of service, the spotlight often falls on individuals—the star server, the charismatic manager, the helpful concierge. But when we look closer, we realize that what truly elevates a customer experience isn't just one person doing their job well.

It's many people, each in their own role, seamlessly working together to create something greater than the sum of their parts.

A great service impression is not delivered in pieces. It flows as a whole. From the moment a customer walks in to the moment they leave, they are being held, guided, and cared for by an invisible net woven by multiple hands of receptionists, housekeepers, chefs, valets, technicians, servers, support staff, and managers. And what makes that net strong is not perfection, but unity.

When every team member sees themselves not just as an individual contributor, but as a co-creator of a shared outcome, something extraordinary happens. The tone changes. The energy shifts. The atmosphere comes alive not with effort, but with harmony.

The best service cultures don't rely on heroic performances. They rely on synchronized effort. Because in the end, lasting impressions aren't made by "me" or "you." They're made by "us.

Chapter 5: Impression Management Is The Key

Let's start with a few familiar moments.

You enter a hotel lobby. The lighting is warm, there's a fragrance in the air, the marble floor shines, and the staff treats you well. No service per say has been delivered yet but you already feel a liking towards the service provider.

Or you walk into any store. The display looks slightly disorganized, the salesperson doesn't look up from his phone, and the billing counter has half-torn posters. Even before you actually get to purchasing the product, you feel a slight hesitation towards the store.

Such instances are concrete proof of a gospel truth in the world of service: Impressions are everything.

They make or break the experience a customer has with a brand; how the customer feels, what they expect, whether they trust, and ultimately, whether they return.

But what exactly is an impression? And why does it matter so much?

The What, When, Why, and How of Impressions

An impression is not just about how something looks. It is about how something feels.

It includes the way a place looks and smells, how attentively someone looks at you, the quality of interaction, and the subtle synergy between design, people, and service flow. It is the sum total of the experience a customer has.

It is formed in the first few seconds but remembered for much longer. Every player in the service sector is in a game of impression building and management. And the stakes are high.

In an ultra-competitive, constantly shifting market where brands are born and buried in weeks, your impression isn't just an aesthetic layer. It is your entire positioning. It determines whether you're seen as just another service provider, or THE provider—one who holds a gold-standard niche in the customer's mind.

An important thing to understand about impressions is that they cannot be accidental. They must always be intentional.

They cannot just happen by chance, or fluctuate based on mood, season, or individual discretion. Great impressions come from a culture of consistency. They are not the result of one moment of brilliance, but the discipline of repeated excellence. It is about living what service experts call the "moment of truth"—the exact instance where customer expectation meets brand delivery.

Impressions wield the power that they do because of the simple truth that people believe what they see. If something looks professional, clean, confident, and composed, they assume that the service behind it will be the same. If something appears sloppy, careless, or chaotic, they begin to doubt the service and the service provider.

In fact, people may give second chances to things they hear, but they rarely unsee what they've seen. For example, if you hear from others that a mall is shabby and ill-maintained, you may still give it a chance and want to check it out for yourself.

But, if you also see it in that state, you will probably never forget that impression and visit it again.

While it is crucial for service providers to pay keen attention to what they are showcasing to customers, it is important to understand that impressions are not optics. A beautiful façade with no substance behind it can fool people once, maybe even twice. However, over time, cracks begin to show.

That's why impressions, just like the service itself, must also have soul. The most lasting service experiences are those that combine form with feeling, and the outer impression with the inner intention.

So, how and when does impression management begin?

It starts long before the customer enters your premises. It begins at the very first point of contact; whether it's an ad on a website, a message on social media, a phone call with a receptionist, or a casual reference in a friend's conversation. That's the real first impression. It's the spark of awareness. It's where curiosity is either ignited or ignored.

That's why businesses must recognize that impression management is not a one-time show. It is a 24x7 responsibility. It's not something the marketing team does, or something the design team takes care of. It's a philosophy that the whole organization lives and breathes because as we have seen, real victory comes only when an entire team works towards a united goal.

To understand impression fully in a service context, one must examine its three pillars: Product, Process, and People.

- **Product**: What you offer must look, feel, and deliver what was promised, no matter how small or big the offering is.

- **Process**: The ease of buying, browsing, navigating, asking for help, lodging feedback, returning products, and getting updates; all of these small processes collectively leave a big imprint.

- **People**: Ultimately, every impression leads back to people—the ones who carry your values forward in live moments. No matter how much you spend on branding, if your people don't *embody* that brand, the impression collapses.

Great service organizations understand this. That's why they don't gamble with impressions. They design them, practice them, and keep them alive across every channel whether—offline, online, and everything in between.

Because in the end, impressions are not masks. They are reflections.

And only those who build their reflections with consistency, care, and authenticity will be remembered.

A Personal Experience: When the Impression Unravels

There's a premium watch brand I have (along with many other customers like me, I'm sure) admired for a long time. Their advertising, their reputation in luxury circles, the way people talked about them—it all painted a picture of timeless class and gold-standard service.

I had been considering buying one of their signature timepieces for a while, and this wasn't just a purchase for me. It was a milestone in my life, and a reward for myself.

As I walked into the store, I had already visualized the exquisite ambience I would see, the kind of welcome I would receive, and the top-notch experience it would be. But the very first thing I saw stopped me in my tracks.

The large signage of the brand was stained. Seven letters in the name, but two of them were dull, almost invisible under layers of dust and faded lighting. I stood there for a moment, unsure if I was at the right place.

This wasn't just any brand; this was supposed to be the brand. The kind that represents legacy and precision. And yet, here I was, staring at a signboard that looked neglected. It was the first dent in my impression. Subtle, but powerful. If this was how they presented themselves from the outside, what did that say about what was happening inside?

Still, I brushed the thought aside and stepped in. The doorman opened the door with grace, and his greeting was warm and poised; just the way it should be in a store of that calibre. I felt a flicker of hope. As I walked in, the service staff were equally polished in their tone and gestures. The receptionist made eye contact, smiled genuinely, and guided me in. I was relieved. This felt more like the brand I had imagined.

But as I moved to the lounge area to wait, the contrast reappeared.

The couch I was asked to sit on had visible stains on the armrest. Some brochures were kept in a disorganized stack on the side table, one of them curling at the edges. I looked around and noticed inconsistency in staff presentation. Some wore polished shoes, others didn't. A few had neat makeup and grooming, while others looked like they had rushed in. It wasn't necessarily offensive but it was not consistent.

And for a brand positioned as elite, these things matter. A luxury experience is not built on just what's sold. It's shaped by how everything feels, looks, sounds, and even smells.

The customer service executive who approached me was polite and said the pieces I had shortlisted were ready. I was happy to engage, but something felt off. There wasn't the energy or excitement you'd expect when a customer is clearly there with the intent to buy.

And then came the tipping point.

I saw the watch being carelessly picked up from a nearby counter and it was brought to me in a shabby tray. There was no proper box, no thought given to the presentation, and it was clear that neither me as a customer nor the product was getting its due respect. As I held the watch, I noticed a faint scratch on the leather strap.

I kept it down gently, thanked the executive, and excused myself. I didn't make the purchase. I didn't even feel the need to explain why. What surprised me was—neither did they ask.

There was no effort to understand what had shifted in my experience. No attempt to read my expression, ask what went wrong, or take any action to improve my experience.

In that one visit, I learned a lesson most service professionals would do well to remember: when you're a high-value brand, your customer doesn't just come to buy a product. They come to experience pride, trust, and certainty. And if any part of that experience feels misaligned—even something as small as a dusty sign or a shoddy presentation —the impression is weakened. And sometimes, it's weakened enough to walk away.

The Real Cost of a Lost First Impression

As it happened with the luxury watch brand that day, a bad first impression meant that they lost the sale they would otherwise have gained from me. But the truth is, that's only the tip of the iceberg. There is a cascade of other problems caused due to this; these are often immeasurable and intangible but the damage they cause to a business is significant.

1. Loss of Trust

Along with the revenue lost from a sale, there is also a loss of trust.

The unspoken belief that "if this is how it starts, it'll only get worse" settles into the customer's mind. And trust, once fractured, is ten times harder to rebuild than it is to establish from the start.

Worse, in today's fast-paced environment, people don't wait around. They'll walk out your door and into someone else's. You don't just lose a customer, but instead, you also hand them over to the competition.

2. Barrier to Brand Loyalty and Relationship Building

A first impression isn't just about the product or service. It's about whether someone feels safe, seen, and valued. When that doesn't happen, they don't return.

What businesses often forget is that loyalty is emotional. It is built on micro-moments of how they were greeted, whether their needs were understood, whether they were made to feel important.

If the first impression fails, the emotional groundwork for loyalty is never laid. And the real loss is that of a potential lifetime relationship, and not just of a one-time buyer.

3. Loss of Advocacy & Negative Publicity

People love to talk about good experiences. They share it with friends, post about it, and recommend it. But here's the flip side: a bad first impression stops the story right there.

The customer won't post a photo, won't recommend you, and won't say, "You have to go there!" You miss out on free, organic brand-building; the kind that no advertising campaign can match.

Even worse, they may broadcast the poor experience. In the current age of social media and reviews, one bad impression can spread faster than a hundred good ones. And a potential advocate becomes a silent critic.

4. Recovery Requires Disproportionate Effort

One of the most draining consequences of a failed first impression is how much effort is needed to recover from it.

Once a customer has decided they don't like your service, it's equivalent to working against gravity. It takes multiple interactions, perhaps from multiple people, with extra measures, discounts, apologies, or escalations just to bring them to a neutral ground.

And even after all that, they may never truly trust again.

Impressions, especially first ones, aren't surface-level. They seep into the customer's memory, shaping what they expect and how they behave. That's why it's not enough to say, "We'll get it right the second time."

Because for many customers, there won't be a second time.

A Pharmacy Visit That Left a Lasting Impression

Now, let's look at the flip side. Through yet another experience of mine, the true meaning of a good impression and how it can be delivered will be emphasized.

I happened to visit a pharmacy once. It was a well-branded store, and I had been there just a couple of days before this visit that I am about to describe. At that time, I had purchased some medicines for one of my relatives who has a migraine problem.

As soon as I walked in, I saw the attendant who had helped me the last time. I understood immediately from his expression and the way he smiled at me that he had recognized me. It immediately made me feel noticed and valued as a customer.

I approached him and before I could say anything, he asked, "Sir, I hope your relative felt better with that migraine tablet? I recollect you had told me that no other medicine was working for them." There was nothing intrusive or fake about the way he spoke, and his genuine concern was evident.

That one line caught me off guard. Not in an uncomfortable way, but in a warm, grounded one. I paused, blinked, and then nodded. I was astonished that he remembered the smallest details of our interaction last time. It told me that our interaction the last time had not just been surface-level, but that he had been truly invested in understanding what I was there for.

As always, my curiosity got the better of me and I asked him the secret of how he remembered that interaction with me.

He gave me a warm smile and said, "Sir, we make it a point to get to know our customers not only as a source of sales, but as individuals. Everyone in this shop will make it a point to truly understand the customer's requirements, make them feel comfortable and reassured, and we pour our heart and soul into every conversation. With that, it takes no effort to remember what the discussion was about!"

That gave me a lot of insight about the culture and systems the service provider had set up. Along with ensuring a good stock of products and a well-maintained store, they had taken a lot of effort into ensuring that the people of the business treated customers well.

Process, product, and people were all delivering gold-standard impressions and that was the reason behind the store's success.

The 3 Cs of Impression Management

Impressions in service are not made in isolation. They are anchored in three essential pillars that hold up the entire architecture of a consistent and credible impression.

Let's explore what each of these truly means:

1. Clarity – Know Who You're Serving, Know What You Stand For

Clarity is the foundation. It's the difference between showing up for a generic customer versus showing up for this customer, at this moment, in this situation.

Clarity means knowing:

- Who your customer is: an elderly couple looking for ease, a busy executive in a rush, a young family trying to stay within a budget.
- What their context is: is it their first time interacting with you, or are they a returning guest with specific preferences?
- And most importantly, what you stand for: what is your role, and what kind of service standard are you representing?

In the absence of clarity, service can become robotic, inconsistent, and often irrelevant.

2. Connectivity – Form Real Human Links

Once you're clear on who you're dealing with, connectivity ensures you're not just serving the person but you're relating to them.

Connectivity is about reading cues, tone, context. It's the part of service that adds soul. It's what makes a guest feel remembered, a client feels valued, or a customer feel seen; not as a ticket number or a payment, but as a person.

This could show up in something as small as a barista remembering your name and your usual order. Or a sales executive asking, "How did the shoes you bought last time work out?" It's about the willingness to engage in real, meaningful interaction.

3. Continuity – Consistency Over Time Builds Trust

The first impression might get the customer's attention. But it is continuity that builds trust. And trust is the most valuable currency in any service relationship.

Continuity means you don't just show up once with excellence. You show up again, and again with consistency, with care, and with credibility. It's about staying true to the impression you have created so that over time, the customer knows what to expect and feels confident coming back.

When service is consistent across time, platforms, and people, it creates a memory of reliability. This is how brands are built- not in one-off great moments, but in sustained excellence.

Bringing the 3 Cs Together: A Seamless Example

We all have some businesses that we regularly obtain service from. It could be your go-to salon, the tailoring shop you visit during every festive season, or the vehicle servicing company that you contact whenever a need arises.

The fact that you have been repeatedly drawn back to these businesses means that they have always given you a good impression. You may have never actively noticed it before, but all three Cs will undoubtedly be at play to offer you the kind of experience that you keep going back for.

Let us see this closely with the example of a salon.

From the moment you enter, the receptionist probably smiles and says, "Good to see you again, it's been a long gap this time! Same haircut and head massage like usual, or something new today?"

That's Clarity—they know who you are and what you usually want.

The hairdresser joins in, warmly asking, "How did that wedding in your family go? You had that trip coming up last time we met, right?"

Another staff member then comes up to you and asks, "Will you have coffee like usual? We will get started on it!"

That's Connectivity—they're not just treating you as another appointment, but as a person with a story and a memory.

The preferred person for the haircut and massage is on time, the products used are the same high quality, the tone of service is relaxed but respectful, just like always.

That's Continuity—the salon has maintained its service rhythm, ensuring that each visit feels reassuringly familiar, yet thoughtfully personal.

By the time you leave, you have got much more than the services than what you originally went in for. And that is what keeps you going back to the salon.

When One of the Cs Is Missing

Let's now explore what happens when one or more of these pillars are absent. Because only when they all come together does a symphony of gold-standard impressions form.

1. Missing Clarity

A customer walks into an upscale mobile store. It's their first time, and they're looking for a business phone with advanced camera and battery specs. The salesperson begins showing them the most expensive flagship model, focusing on features that don't match the customer's actual needs.

The customer feels like they're being sold to and not served. The lack of clarity in understanding the customer's requirement damages the impression. The interaction may still feel professional, but not purposeful.

2. Missing Connectivity

A woman visits a diagnostic lab for her third appointment in two months. Despite her frequent visits, every time she comes, she's asked for her name, details, and ID proof without so much as a "welcome back."

The process is efficient. The staff is technically competent. But it all feels cold.

There is no human connection and the entire experience is sterile. A small amount of warmth or memory of her previous visits could have created a lasting impression of care and comfort.

3. Missing Continuity

A guest checks into a five-star hotel where her first two stays were exceptional. Warm staff, seamless room service, and personal touches like a welcome note. But over the next two visits, everything is off.

The check-in feels rushed, the staff seems new and uninformed, the service is delayed, the rooms are not cleaned up to the usual expectation. Despite earlier experiences, she begins to doubt the brand.

Because while clarity and connectivity were once present, the lack of continuity breaks trust.

Crafting Consistent Impressions

We've already seen how Process, Product, and People together shape the way a service is experienced. But knowing this is only the first step. The real challenge, and the real opportunity, lies in making sure each of these three pillars consistently supports the impression that the business wants to create.

We will now look at each one more closely, exploring practical ways to strengthen them so that every interaction, every touchpoint, reflects the same high standard, every single time.

Through the Power of Process

Unlike people or products, which can occasionally falter or fluctuate, processes are designed to ensure consistency, predictability, and reliability. In the context of impression management, the process is not a back-end, mechanical entity. It's the invisible thread that ties together every customer interaction, ensuring that what a customer feels once, they continue to feel every time.

1. Process is the Blueprint Behind the Brand Experience

When you enter a luxury spa, you expect the same welcome each time; not because the receptionist remembers you, but because the process mandates that welcome.

Process turns good intentions into replicable actions. It ensures that:

- The tone of greeting matches the brand's personality.
- The waiting area is always clean and calming.
- The water is served at just the right temperature.
- Feedback is collected after every visit.

2. Process Sets the Standard Before the People Step In

A lot of businesses over-rely on their "star performers." But what happens when they are on leave, transferred, or replaced? That's where a strong process steps in.

A well-defined service process ensures that no matter who is on duty, the service impression is the same. That includes:

- Pre-written scripts for greetings and farewells.
- Visual checklists for cleanliness or quality.
- Time protocols for response and redressal.

- Non-negotiables around tone, grooming, and customer courtesy.

3. Process Minimizes Human Errors and Emotional Gaps

Even the best of employees have bad days. They may be tired, distracted, or emotionally distant. But the process doesn't get tired.

That's why a brand's impression should not depend on a person's emotional state, but rather on the system that surrounds them. For instance:

- If an airline ground staff is stressed, the process ensures that the boarding announcements, gate changes, and delay communications still happen on time.
- If a hotel receptionist is swamped, the process of automated guest alerts, bellboy assistance, and welcome drinks still create a good impression.

Process becomes a safety net. It catches what may otherwise fall through the cracks of human inconsistency.

4. Process Must Be Realistic, Not Robotic

A good process never feels like a checklist. It should enhance the experience, not interrupt it.

Customers can always sense when someone is just going through the motions. So, while the process should provide structure, it must also allow for:

- Personalization within the framework (e.g., letting a hotel staff add a handwritten note for returning guests).

- Flexibility for situational decisions (e.g., waiving off a small charge for a regular customer without managerial approval).
- Empowerment to use discretion while still following protocol.

5. The Process Must Be Aligned with the Brand's Promise

Every process should echo the brand's identity. If a brand promises luxury, warmth, speed, or care, the process must reflect that. This alignment ensures that the process is not just efficient but also emotionally resonant.

For example, a luxury car showroom's service process should include valet parking, scented waiting areas, and personalized coffee preferences.

It's not just about what the customer receives, but how it matches what they expected from your brand.

Through the Power of Product

Unlike processes, which work quietly in the background, products stand front and center. They are the tangible proof of what a brand promises. In impression management, a product is far more than the item or service being sold; it is the embodiment of the brand's standards, values, and attention to detail. Every time a customer experiences it, the product should reaffirm the trust they've placed in you, delivering not just functionality, but the feeling and quality they've come to expect.

1. The Product Must Reflect Consistency and Quality

One great product experience is a good impression. But repeated great product experiences create loyalty and advocacy. Consistency in quality is what turns a first-time visitor into a repeat customer and a repeat customer into a loyalist.

Let's say someone walks into a bakery and falls in love with the croissant. If the next time it's dry, or burnt, or unavailable, the impression is broken. A customer who comes to a spa and gets a great massage today but a rushed, inattentive service next month starts doubting the brand.

That's why brands must:

- Define clear quality benchmarks for every product.
- Have quality control systems to regularly test the consistency.
- Use feedback loops to tweak and improve the product based on real user experience.

A strong product offering is not made in the factory or in the back kitchen alone. It is made in the repetition of experience that feels just as good each time.

2. The Product Must Match the Positioning

This is where impression and expectation collide. The product has to not only be good, but it has to feel appropriate for the price, positioning, and promise made by the brand.

If a high-end furniture brand delivers a piece that squeaks or chips easily, no matter how beautiful the showroom or how helpful the staff, the experience feels hollow.

This means the product should:

- Reflect the aesthetic, performance, and depth expected at that brand level.
- Be presented with the same care as its creation. (A great watch deserves a pristine case, not a scratched tray.)
- Be in line with the narrative the business is telling about itself.

A mismatch between product and positioning is like a beautiful cover on a disappointing book; it erodes long-term trust.

3. The Product is Also How It's Delivered and Supported

In the world of service, the product is not just the item or end-result. It includes how it is handed over, explained, supported, and maintained. This is often where businesses lose out on creating a lasting impression.

For example, when a customer buys a premium camera. The product includes the manual clarity, the ease of setup, and the availability of tech support.

Even in the case of non-physical products, like therapy sessions, coaching programs, or design consultations—the documentation, follow-ups, and closure rituals are part of the product impression.

A great impression comes from complete delivery; not just the core product, but everything that surrounds and supports it.

Through the Power of People

At the heart of every impression lies the human touch. Processes may guide the flow and products may represent the promise, but it is people who breathe life into both. They are the voice, the smile, the problem-solvers, and the memory-makers who carry the brand into the customer's mind and heart.

1. People Are the Face of the Brand

In most service settings, the first real impression a customer gets is through a person—not the product, not the process.

Even before the customer sees the offering or experiences the service, they are already forming judgments about professionalism, warmth, efficiency, attention. That's why people in a service business must be:

- Properly trained
- Genuinely engaged
- And emotionally attuned to how they carry the brand in every gesture.

A warm greeting, a confident posture, a helpful tone; these are not just courtesies but rather are impression markers.

2. People Reflect the Culture and Standards of the Business

Every person in an organization mirrors its internal culture. If the culture is careless, people will behave carelessly. If it is respectful and empowering, people carry that same energy forward.

That's why people need not just technical training, but also:

- Cultural onboarding
- Soft skills development
- And regular values reinforcement sessions

They must know what kind of experience they are supposed to represent because every human interaction either lifts the brand or lowers it.

3. Train Beyond the Job Description

Businesses require to go beyond technical skills and teach service teams how to deliver the experience in a way that reflects the brand's personality and values. This includes tone, body language, empathy, and micro-interactions that customers remember.

For example, cashiers are taught not just to scan items quickly but to maintain friendly eye contact, acknowledge waiting customers, and hand over purchases in a neat, respectful way.

Similarly, reception staff at a clinic are trained to greet patients warmly, use their names, and offer reassurance if they seem anxious, instead of treating them like just another file in the system.

4. Maintain Consistent Grooming and Presentation Standards

Ensure every staff member reflects a polished, professional, and brand-aligned appearance so the customer's first visual impression matches the service promise.

Cafes ensure that their baristas wear clean aprons, keep hair neatly tied back, and ensure name badges are visible so that customers instantly recognize a consistent standard, even during rush hours.

In luxury stores, sales associates maintain a clean and minimal look, with subtle accessories and fragrances, so the focus stays on the product and the atmosphere feels elevated.

These examples show how the maintenance of grooming and presentation standards of people elevate the impression of the business. These are small and easily implementable changes, but they will have a significantly large impact.

Conclusion: The Impression That Lasts

Every person walking into a service space today is not just looking for a transaction. They're silently asking a fundamental question: Will this experience make me feel seen, respected, and valued?

And the answer begins forming long before a product is bought or a service is consumed.

From the very first moment of contact—whether it's a signboard, a website, a phone call, or a doorman—impressions begin to layer. And those layers stack up quickly.

A slightly careless touch, an unpolished interaction, or a missing smile may seem small at the moment, but in the customer's mind, it shapes the narrative. And in a world where attention spans are short and expectations are high, there is rarely a second chance to make that first impression count.

What truly separates good from great in the service world is not just technical excellence, but emotional resonance. It's the ability of the brand—through every individual who represents it—to make the customer feel like they matter.

Because in the end, you don't just remember what you bought or how long it took. All that you remember how it felt.

That feeling is the impression. That impression is your brand.

And that brand is built every single day, by every single person, in every single moment of truth.

Chapter 6: Blending Compassion with Curiosity

How Curiosity & Compassion Transform a Service Experience

Back when I was in-charge of a sizable team, there was a small task I would take up every 2 or 3 weeks. I used to visit a small store that sold greeting cards saying 'Great Job!', 'Thank You!', or 'Congratulations!' to hand out to my team. It was a routine thing to do. And yet, something that I saw and felt in that shop transformed it into a special experience. It made me want to keep going back.

There was an errand boy at the shop. I would see him moving between aisles with a broom in one hand and a stack of boxes in the other. He always greeted me with a smile, one that showed his sincerity and genuineness.

One of the main reasons why I had chosen that particular shop went beyond the quality of the product. It was the way the place functioned. Each category was always neatly arranged, never mixed up, and the stands looked as though someone had taken extra care to make sure the sections felt inviting. One day, the owner told me it was that same errand boy who quietly took responsibility for keeping the cards organised. It struck me because this wasn't his "main" job. He wasn't the one selling or upselling, but he treated the display as if it was his personal project. It told me that he truly cared about every customer walking through the door.

Since I always went on my lunch break, I had one eye on my watch constantly. I had never imagined that it would even be noticeable to anyone, but it was. All because someone was really looking out for me. One day when I was there, the errand boy came up to me and said, "I know you're short on time, sir. I have a new assortment for you. It will help you save time and find what you're looking for."

He had observed that small gesture of mine over time and gone a step beyond to make sure I have a convenient shopping experience. Then, while I was looking through the stock, he asked me, "Sir, I wanted to ask the reason why you need these cards? If I know that, I can try to keep aside a similar assortment ready for you the next time you come."

I left the shop incredibly impressed.

In that moment, I realised he was showing two rare but vital qualities: curiosity—the interest to understand who his customers were beyond the transaction—and compassion—the willingness to adjust his own role to make my experience better.

The DNA of Exceptional Service

In the service world, there's a truth so fundamental that it has outlived trends, technologies, and even entire industries: **The customer is the reason you exist.**

Over the years, we've dressed it up in many ways like "*Customer is king,*" "*We put the customer first,*" "*We serve with a smile*"—but underneath every slogan is the same reality. If there is no customer, there is no business. And in a customer service environment, this is not just a mission statement you hang on a wall; it's the DNA that should run through every single person who interacts with or influences the customer's experience.

But knowing this truth and living it are two very different things. The marketplace today is not what it was even a decade ago. The pace is faster, the competition is sharper, and the customer's mindset has evolved. In the past, people often came with needs. Today, customers arrive not just with needs, but with wants, expectations, opinions, and a certain curiosity of their own. They have already compared you with your competitors before stepping in. They carry a belief about your brand—sometimes from advertising, sometimes from word-of-mouth—and they arrive with an expectation to see that belief validated.

This is why service today cannot be about going through the motions. The real power lies in something deeper, something more human: Compassion and Curiosity. As I experienced personally in that shop, these are complete game-changers for any service experience.

Compassion is the ability to see beyond the transaction and really look at the person. It means regarding every customer as a human being with a story, a reason for being here, and possibly an unspoken need. It is the awareness that you are there only because of the customer, because they have given you their time, trust, and business. Compassion means you care enough to notice when someone is rushed, when they seem anxious, or when they are unfamiliar with how things work. It's about thinking, "What can I do right now to make this easier, better, smoother for them?"

Curiosity, on the other hand, is what keeps service alive, relevant, and dynamic. It's not about being nosy or asking inquisitive questions that may make a customer uncomfortable. It's about striking that right balance in the way you ask questions and correctly modulating your enthusiasm, as we have previously discussed in detail. At the heart of it is a genuine interest in the person in front of you. Curiosity is the instinct that makes you ask the right questions—not just to close a sale or finish a task, but to truly understand what will serve the customer best. It's what turns a routine transaction into a meaningful interaction. And, often, it's what helps you uncover needs that the customer didn't even know they had, or solve problems before they become complaints.

In a way, compassion is the heart of service, and curiosity is the mind. One without the other leaves the experience incomplete.

Compassion without curiosity can make you kind but ineffective; you care, but you're not actively seeking to improve or personalise the service. Curiosity without compassion can make you efficient but cold; you find solutions, but without warmth or understanding, the experience feels transactional. Together, they create the perfect balance: the emotional connection that makes customers feel valued, and the honest engagement that makes them feel understood.

And here's the thing—no amount of automation, no AI-driven chatbot, no streamlined self-service portal can truly replicate this human combination. Technology can answer queries, process payments, even anticipate certain needs, but it cannot feel for a customer, and it cannot be genuinely curious about their unique circumstances. That's why, in the long run, the people who will thrive in service are the ones who carry these two traits in their DNA. They are the ones who remain relevant in a changing market, who can adapt to new customer behaviours, who can be consistent with the best practices of the past while staying tuned to the emerging needs of the future.

Let's understand this better with the help of an example.

How Compassion and Curiosity Transform Customer Moments

When a service professional has these qualities in their DNA, they carry an internal compass that constantly points toward serving the customer well. They instinctively operate from the belief, *"I am here because of the customer, not the other way around."*

In a world where technology can increasingly replace functional roles, these human traits are what keep service professionals relevant, valued, and irreplaceable. AI can answer questions, but it cannot feel what the other person feels—it cannot sense the subtle frustration in a voice, the hesitation in a request, or the relief in a customer's "thank you."

Consider an airport scenario where due to an unavoidable and unexpected development, flights are being delayed.

Airports now have sophisticated systems to keep passengers updated: SMS alerts, gate display screens, and AVR systems to efficiently answer all queries. From a functional perspective, the customer is "informed."

But imagine a passenger who's not just concerned about the departure time, but about making a tight connection, or getting home to a sick family member, or arriving in time for an important meeting. This is where the type of human interaction available to them changes everything.

Imagine if passengers only have a chatbot to interact with. The responses are quick and accurate; exact gate numbers, estimated boarding times, baggage claim instructions, and all other details are provided. But, the conversation is emotionally empty. It answers the "what" but ignores the "why it matters."

That's where the human connect comes in. And not just any human connects, but one that is driven by the two most important traits in service.

Let us now imagine a scenario where a passenger does connect with a person, but one who is reading from a rigid script, without bringing any real human connection there. The tone is polite but mechanical, with standard phrases like, "We apologize for the inconvenience" repeated verbatim. The customer feels they are speaking to a human-shaped computer.

The customer is probably not just concerned about the technicalities, which the script accurately covers. Instead, they are looking for some understanding about their situation; perhaps they have a tight window to make a connection elsewhere, or have to get home to a sick family member, or arrive in time for some important event. This is where human interaction that's full of curiosity and compassion will come to the rescue.

A person who is there to listen to the passenger. Someone who will listen more than speaking, allowing the customer to explain their situation in their own words. Then they ask a simple but powerful question: "Can you tell me what's most important for you to reach your destination on time?"

This opens the door to understanding the real stakes. Perhaps the passenger has a 40-minute layover in another city, or they're traveling with a child who needs medication upon arrival, or they have an important personal commitment they cannot miss.

With this knowledge, the representative can act meaningfully—checking alternative connections, prioritizing the passenger for a faster boarding process, coordinating with ground staff, or even suggesting adjustments that minimize stress.

The difference is palpable. The customer walks away thinking, "*They really cared about my problem.*"

When human compassion and curiosity are absent, interactions slip into a purely transactional mode. Information is exchanged, but no relationship is built. The customer may still get to their destination, but the impression of the brand remains neutral, or worse- negative.

Once that impression is lost, no amount of marketing slogans can easily win it back. Because, if you recollect, impressions are the lifeline for any business to thrive.

When they are present, however, even a frustrating situation like a delayed flight can become an opportunity to deepen loyalty. Customers remember how you made them feel, and they tell others about it. This is why, in any service organization, people are not just a "department"—they are the living, breathing representation of the brand.

When you approach service with both compassion and curiosity, you are no longer just "doing your job". You are crafting an experience. You're building a bridge between the customer's expectations and the reality you deliver.

And in a world where brands are constantly competing for attention, that bridge is often the deciding factor between someone becoming a loyal advocate or a one-time visitor who never returns.

Facets of Compassion in Service

Compassion in a service environment is never just about feeling sorry for someone or extending kindness when it's convenient. It is about embedding care into the very fabric of every interaction, so it becomes second nature. True compassion is active, deliberate, and impactful. It not only transforms a single customer's experience but influences the entire culture of service delivery. Below are the key facets that bring this quality to life in practical, measurable ways.

1. The Ripple Effect of Compassion

A small gesture of care can extend far beyond the immediate moment. Like a single stone can create a ripple effect that covers a large water body's surface, even one act of compassion can make a longstanding difference. In a busy supermarket, a cashier spots an elderly customer struggling to pack groceries while managing a walking stick. The cashier leaves the till for a moment to help, and soon another team member joins in to carry the bags to the customer's car. A couple of waiting customers also helped pick up items that had rolled out of a bag. That single moment, witnessed by dozens, quietly tells everyone present that kindness is part of the store's culture.

2. Balancing Empathy with Efficiency

Empathy without action can feel hollow, and efficiency without empathy can feel cold. The magic lies in striking a balance—listening to the customer's concern with genuine care while also moving quickly to address it.

When a hotel guest complains that their room is too cold late at night, the staff member doesn't just send someone hours later to check the air conditioning. They listen attentively, empathize with the discomfort, offer an immediate portable heater, and arrange for a full maintenance check in the morning. In doing so, they combine emotional intelligence with practical action, ensuring the guest feels cared for and their problem resolved quickly.

3. Personalization Through Attentive Care

Compassion shines when service is tailored to the individual rather than delivered as a generic transaction. This can be as simple as remembering a returning customer's name, favorite product, or previous request. A café barista who says, "The usual cappuccino with oat milk?" not only saves the customer time but also communicates that they are recognized and valued.

Consider the example of a pharmacy assistant who notices that a regular customer usually buys supplements for joint pain. On their next visit, the assistant mentions a new formulation that might work better, explaining the differences without any sales pressure. The customer not only appreciates the advice but also feels the assistant genuinely cares about their well-being.

4. Proactive Protection of Customer Comfort

The most impressive acts of compassion often happen before a problem arises. Think of an airline crew offering blankets before passengers ask, or a spa receptionist explaining treatment options in detail to reduce a first-time guest's anxiety. These gestures show an understanding of customer needs before they are voiced, signalling that the business prioritizes comfort, trust, and security at every stage.

5. Consistency of Warmth Across All Touchpoints

Compassion loses its strength when it's sporadic. Remember how important consistency is in delivering an impression? In the same manner, compassion must be consistently embodied to truly become a part of the service's culture.

A customer should feel the same level of care whether interacting with a live agent on a phone call, walking into a store, or chatting via an online helpdesk. Inconsistent compassion creates confusion—was that one exceptional staff member an anomaly, or is the business truly customer-first? Building systems, training, and culture that reinforce warmth at every touchpoint ensures the customer never has to guess.

6. Compassion Under Pressure

It's easy to be compassionate on a slow day when everything is going right; the real test is when tensions rise. Whether it's handling a delayed order, a technical glitch, or an irate customer, staying calm, patient, and solution-oriented is what sets true professionals apart. In these moments, compassion is not weakness—it's the very thing that can de-escalate a situation, salvage a relationship, and even turn an unhappy customer into an advocate.

7. Empowering Others Through Compassion

Compassion isn't limited to customer-facing interactions. When team members extend understanding, patience, and support to one another, it creates a stronger internal culture. A compassionate manager who supports a team member through personal difficulties fosters loyalty, reduces burnout, and indirectly ensures better service to customers. Compassion within the team is the foundation for compassion towards customers.

Facets of Curiosity in Service

Curiosity in a service role is a professional superpower. It pushes the service provider to look beyond surface requests, listen beyond rehearsed responses, and connect beyond the transaction. When nurtured deliberately, curiosity turns an ordinary service exchange into something that leaves the customer thinking, *"They really understood me."* Below are the many ways curiosity manifests and why it matters.

1. Curiosity as a Problem-Solving Tool

Many customer issues are like icebergs; you can only see a fraction of how deep the problem really runs. Curiosity prompts the service professional to probe gently, peeling back the layers until they reach the true cause. This is not about asking endless questions for the sake of it; it's about purposeful inquiry that leads to accurate solutions.

For instance, instead of a flat "Do you want a refund?", a curious mind asks, "What would the best resolution look like for you?" This shifts the conversation from a one-size-fits-all answer to a tailored solution.

Imagine a customer brings a smartphone into a service center complaining about poor battery life. A quick-fix mindset might swap out the battery and send them on their way. But a curious technician asks, "When does it drain the fastest—when you're on calls, streaming videos, or using certain apps?" The answer reveals that a recent app update is consuming power in the background.

Instead of unnecessary hardware replacement, the technician solves the actual problem and earns the customer's trust for life.

2. Curiosity for Anticipating Needs

Great service is often remembered not for what was asked but for what was offered without being asked. Curiosity plays a critical role here. It drives the professional to observe patterns, notice details, and connect dots that others miss.

Consider a luxury hotel scenario. A guest requests an extra pillow. A purely procedural employee delivers one. But a curious staff member notices the baby cot in the room and thinks, "They might need something for the baby too." Moments later, along with the pillow, they bring extra infant-safe blankets. This small act, born from curiosity, transforms a standard delivery into a moment of thoughtful care.

3. Curiosity that Drives Learning

In service industries, situations evolve, products change, and customer expectations shift. Curious professionals don't wait for formal training; they ask, research, and learn in real time. They talk to colleagues from other departments, experiment with systems, and keep their knowledge fresh.

This means that when a customer throws an unexpected question— "Do you stock the new eco-friendly variant of this product?"—they can answer confidently or at least know exactly where to find the information. Over time, this makes them a go-to person for both customers and peers.

4. Curiosity as a Connector

At its heart, curiosity is about people, not just problems. It's about wanting to know more. Not in a nosy way, but in a way that says, "I'm interested in your story." This creates a thread that ties one interaction to the next, making the customer feel recognized rather than processed.

A regular at a coffee shop orders the same latte every morning. One day, the barista casually asks, "I've always wondered—what makes this your go-to drink?" This sparks a short story about a trip to Colombia years ago. The next week, the barista uses Colombian beans for the brew and says, "a complimentary biscotti with their coffee, saying, "Just a little taste of Colombia for you." That moment is not just service; it's connection.

5. Curiosity that Fuels Innovation

Many service improvements start with one simple question: "Why is it done this way?" A curious professional doesn't blindly follow outdated processes; they challenge them, looking for better, faster, or more customer-friendly options.

For example, in a retail store, a floor associate might notice customers often put certain products back because they can't find prices easily. Instead of shrugging, they suggest a new shelf labelling system. The result? Fewer abandoned items, faster decision-making for customers, and higher sales.

6. Curiosity to Improve the Customer's Journey

Customer experience is a chain of touchpoints, and a weak link anywhere can ruin the whole impression. Curious service providers study the journey holistically, asking themselves, "Where could frustration creep in?" and "What could make this smoother?"

An airline service rep notices that passengers at the gate frequently ask about charging points. Instead of simply pointing them in the right direction each time, they propose adding a "charging station map" link in the pre-boarding email. This tiny innovation improves convenience for thousands of travellers without increasing staff workload.

7. Curiosity that Builds Empathy

The most valuable form of curiosity in service is the one that leads to understanding—not just what happened, but why it matters. It's about uncovering the emotional weight behind a request.

A guest complaining about a noisy hotel room might not just be "picky"; perhaps they are recovering from surgery and desperately need rest. By asking, "Is there anything specific making this noise more of a concern for you?" the staff learns the real reason and can act with urgency. This kind of curiosity bridges the gap between service and care.

Training Compassion and Curiosity – How Businesses Can Embed These Traits in Their Team Culture

Compassion and curiosity are not ornamental qualities in service, but are operational necessities. While technical competence can be taught through structured training, the instinct to empathize and the urge to know more come from a deeper place. For a business to truly weave these into its culture, it must start at the very beginning—hiring—and then sustain them through every stage of an employee's journey, especially in high-pressure service contexts where these values are most tested.

1. Hiring for Attitude Over Skill

When recruiting for service roles, many organizations default to scanning résumés for years of experience, product knowledge, or technical certifications. While these are important, they rarely predict how a person will handle a frustrated customer, anticipate unspoken needs, or go the extra mile to resolve a problem.

Skills can be taught in weeks; attitude is often ingrained over years. An applicant with an innate warmth, patience, and genuine interest in people can be trained to use a booking system, but someone who lacks these qualities will struggle to turn mechanical transactions into meaningful interactions, no matter how technically proficient they are.

A hotel, for example, might hire a front-desk candidate who has never worked in hospitality but naturally makes people feel at ease within moments of meeting them. In contrast, an applicant with a decade of front-desk experience but a curt, dismissive tone may pass technical tests yet fail to inspire guest loyalty.

During interviews, include scenario-based questions that reveal empathy and curiosity, such as:

- "Tell me about a time you went out of your way to help someone without being asked."
- "What's a recent situation where asking the right question changed the outcome?"

2. Embedding a People-First Mindset in Training

Once the right people are hired, onboarding should do more than explain processes. It should anchor them in the why. Every operational policy should be linked to the ultimate goal of making the customer feel heard, respected, and cared for.

Instead of teaching returns policy purely as a step-by-step script, trainers can show how a compassionate approach ("I understand this didn't work for you—let's see how we can fix that") changes the customer's emotional state, which in turn shapes their willingness to shop again.

Think of service employees as stage actors. The script (process) matters, but the tone, expression, and improvisation (compassion and curiosity) are what make the audience applaud.

3. Sustaining the Mindset in High-Pressure Environments

In peak seasons, during system outages, or when handling a wave of customer complaints, it's easy for staff to default to survival mode—minimizing conversations, sticking rigidly to scripts, and focusing solely on clearing the queue. But these are the moments that define a brand's reputation.

A customer might forgive a delay if they sense the service provider genuinely cares. But a rushed, robotic interaction in a crisis can cement a negative impression that outweighs years of good service.

Consider an airport check-in desk during multiple flight cancellations. The rep who says, "Next passenger, please," without looking up is processing transactions. The rep who greets each traveler with, "I can see this has been a frustrating day—let's see what I can do to make this easier for you," is managing impressions, building loyalty, and protecting the brand's image under stress.

Here are a few ways that service businesses can empower their people for this mindset:

- Rotate staff so they have micro-breaks to recharge between high-intensity interactions.
- Provide them with decision-making authority to offer small but impactful gestures—a free beverage, a seat upgrade, or expedited boarding. These acts both reduce customer stress and remind employees of the human purpose behind their work.

4. Reinforcing Through Recognition and Storytelling

Embedding compassion and curiosity in culture requires constant reinforcement. Recognizing employees who embody these traits—through peer nominations, customer feedback highlights, or leadership shout-outs—signals that the company values them as much as meeting sales or service KPIs.

A retail chain might start each morning briefing with "Customer Moments of the Day" from the previous day, spotlighting instances where an employee's curiosity uncovered a hidden need or compassion diffused a tense situation. This storytelling not only reinforces desired behavior but also inspires others to adopt the same mindset.

The ROI of Compassion & Curiosity in Service

In service businesses, the return on investment isn't measured only in revenue or efficiency but also in emotions. Compassion and curiosity may seem like intangible traits, but their effects ripple through every layer of a business, shaping customer perception, team morale, and long-term brand equity.

When a customer feels genuinely cared for, they remember it. They come back, they tell others, and they develop a trust that is difficult for competitors to break. Similarly, when employees work in an environment that values their humanity, they give more of themselves, remain loyal longer, and contribute to a healthier workplace culture. The emotional ROI of service is, therefore, not just about "being nice"—it's about generating tangible business value through human connection.

1. Reduced Customer Churn

Customer churn is often viewed as a purely competitive or price-driven problem, but in reality, it's deeply emotional. People don't just stay with a brand because of the product or service—they stay because of the way it makes them feel. Compassion ensures that customers feel valued beyond their monetary worth, while curiosity ensures that their evolving needs are understood and addressed. When customers sense that a brand is paying attention to their specific preferences and challenges, they begin to view the relationship as personal rather than transactional. This emotional investment makes them far less likely to walk away, even if a competitor offers similar features or lower prices.

For example, a local café that remembers a customer's regular order and asks about their recent vacation may be selling the same coffee as the chain down the street, but the emotional familiarity creates a sense of belonging that no loyalty card can replicate.

2. Better Reviews and Word-of-Mouth Advocacy

Modern customers aren't shy about sharing their experiences online or with their personal networks. What they choose to share, however, depends entirely on the emotional imprint left on them. Compassion leaves them feeling cared for in moments that mattered; curiosity makes them feel understood and important. These feelings naturally lead to richer, more personal reviews that carry weight with future customers.

Unlike generic feedback, which quickly blends into the background, emotionally charged stories stick in the minds of potential buyers, effectively turning loyal customers into powerful brand ambassadors without any extra marketing spend.

It's the difference between a review that says "Good service" and one that says, "The staff noticed I was struggling with my heavy bag and offered to carry it to my car without me asking. I've never experienced that kind of kindness in a store before." The latter paints a story, and stories sell.

3. Stronger Community Presence

A brand that operates with compassion and curiosity doesn't just serve customers. It becomes part of their daily lives. This means the business is not perceived as a faceless provider but as a familiar, reliable participant in the community's rhythm. Compassion allows businesses to identify with the struggles, joys, and milestones of the people they serve, while curiosity helps them anticipate changes in local needs and trends. Over time, this positioning as a trusted, human presence builds a level of goodwill that advertising dollars alone cannot buy.

Consider a small-town hardware store that takes the time to guide a young couple through their first home repair, even though the sale is minimal, may later be recommended to the entire street. Over time, such actions cement the brand as a trusted local partner rather than a faceless seller.

4. Increased Employee Retention

For employees, the culture they work in often matters just as much, if not more, than the product or service being sold. When a workplace encourages them to be compassionate and curious in their interactions, it signals that emotional intelligence is valued just as much as technical competence. This kind of environment makes employees feel respected and trusted, which translates to pride in their work and a sense of belonging. Over time, this reduces turnover rates because staff don't just work for a paycheck; they work for a cause they believe in and a team that believes in them.

A call center that celebrates "Customer Wins" stories at weekly meetings not only keeps morale high but also reinforces the idea that employees are not just handling cases. They're making a difference in people's lives.

5. Resilience in High-Pressure Situations

High-pressure environments, such as peak sales seasons, crises, or customer complaints, are often where the real test of service culture lies. Employees who have compassion in their DNA respond to stress with empathy, which calms tense situations rather than escalating them. Curiosity enables them to investigate problems deeply rather than relying on surface-level fixes. Together, these traits give staff the ability to adapt quickly, think creatively, and maintain a human connection with customers even when under intense pressure, thereby turning potential service failures into opportunities for brand loyalty.

During a holiday rush, a retail associate who approaches a long queue with light humor, empathy for customers' wait, and curiosity about their needs creates a positive energy in the room, thereby turning a stressful environment into a shared experience.

6. The Compound Effect on Brand Loyalty

When both customers and employees consistently experience compassion and curiosity, a self-reinforcing cycle forms. Customers reward the brand with repeat business, referrals, and advocacy; employees, in turn, feel the impact of their work and are motivated to keep delivering at the same high level. Over time, this builds a resilient, loyal customer base that isn't easily swayed by competitors. This loyalty is not just about habit—it's rooted in trust, emotional connection, and the belief that the brand genuinely has their best interests at heart.

Conclusion: Service That Lasts Beyond the Moment

In the end, great service is not just about delivering a product, fixing a problem, or fulfilling a request. It is about creating moments that people carry with them; moments shaped by clarity, connectivity, and continuity, and powered by the deeper forces of compassion and curiosity. Processes may ensure that the service runs like clockwork, products may speak for the brand's quality, and people may bring it all to life. However, without the human ability to care and the willingness to explore, the experience will always fall short of its potential.

Compassion keeps us grounded in the truth that every interaction is with a real person; someone with their own pressures, joys, and fears. Curiosity ensures we do not just meet their stated need but understand the bigger picture behind it, anticipating ways to help that they may not have even considered. Together, these traits transform routine exchanges into memorable connections and transactional relationships into enduring loyalty.

The businesses that master this balance reap rewards far beyond revenue. They earn the trust of their customers, the pride of their employees, and the strength of a brand presence that cannot be faked or forced. And in a marketplace where technology is closing the gap on speed, accuracy, and convenience, the emotional depth of human-led service becomes the true competitive advantage.

When compassion and curiosity become part of a company's DNA—woven into every process, every product touchpoint, and every person who represents the brand—service is no longer something you deliver. It becomes something you embody. And that is the kind of impression that lasts long after the interaction is over.

Chapter 7: Emotion is The Real Strength

Technological advancements in today's age are happening at an astonishing pace. Businesses now have tools for providing real-time data, predicting trends, and insights, automating responses faster than any human ever could provide. And this tech has made its way into every sphere of our lives, including the service industry. But even though it has made its way in, can it fully replace the human touch? No.

Why is it so? After all, machines and software are programmable to become much more efficient and accurate than humans can be. Why, then, are people still the heart and soul of service?

That's because despite all the leaps and bounds that technology has made, it can never replicate a USP that humans inherently possess. That USP is emotion.

A customer does not choose a brand only because of its efficiency, price, or innovation. The choice is purely based on how the brand makes them feel and how it emotionally resonates with the brand. When a customer feels an emotional attachment to a brand, the bond goes far deeper than a transaction. It becomes intimate, personal, and naturally becomes enduring too.

This is why service professionals, from frontline staff to top-level leadership, must treat emotion as their greatest strength. Without it, the finest systems will feel cold. With it, even slight imperfections can be forgiven because there's a deeper connect and stronger loyalty.

Emotion as Strength

Having emotion as strength means carrying the soul of service into every interaction. It is about ensuring that respect, empathy, and human connection remain at the center, regardless of the tools or processes involved.

That's why emotions are the biggest strength and strongest asset of any person involved in service.

Emotional strength is all about balance. A service person cannot allow their personal stress or fatigue to leak into the customer interaction, but they also cannot become so detached that their responses feel robotic. The key lies in measured emotion; responding with warmth, empathy, and patience while maintaining composure.

Let's revisit the airport example that we considered earlier. For a passenger whose flight is delayed, the issue is deeply personal and centered around themself only. For the service agent, however, this may be the hundredth such complaint of the day. The difference between mechanical service and emotional service lies in how the agent manages their own feelings. A script-driven, flat-toned apology leaves the passenger feeling like just another case. But an emotionally intelligent response by listening, empathizing, and saying, "I can imagine this must be stressful, let me see what I can do to help," creates reassurance. It transforms frustration into trust and adds a layer of emotional depth to the exchange, even if the delay itself cannot be resolved.

But there's a flip side too.

Because emotions are such a potent way to build lasting bonds, they can easily become an undoing too. Despite being so powerful, they are also fragile. When a customer feels cared for, they may forgive small mistakes like an order arriving late, or a call not returned immediately, because the relationship feels strong. But if the emotional connection is missing, even a small error becomes a deal-breaker.

This is why leading brands sometimes lose their position at the top. It's because somewhere along the way, customers no longer feel the same connection. Once that intimacy breaks, rebuilding it is extremely challenging, if not impossible. A brand can repair a technical error or adjust a pricing model, but regaining lost trust at an emotional level is a far steeper climb.

Think of it as a glass bridge. When intact, it is strong, beautiful, and capable of carrying enormous weight. But if it cracks even in one small section, the sense of safety is gone. The customer may continue to walk on it for a while, but the bond of trust is shattered. Emotional bonds in service work the same way: powerful when cared for, but vulnerable if neglected in even the slightest sense.

Another critical truth about emotion in service is that every customer's need is unique. No two individuals arrive with the same expectations, the same urgency, or the same context. Generic service, where everyone is treated in exactly the same way, misses this fact and risks alienating customers.

A customer might come in anxious, another joyful, another hurried. Emotional intelligence demands that the service professional adapts their approach to the situation at hand. This is what made the doorman at that café I talked about earlier so memorable; he did not greet people like a task to be checked off but like a host welcoming someone into his own space. The warmth of his greeting matched the customer's need for acknowledgment and belonging.

Similarly, the errand boy in the greeting card shop did not treat his role as mechanical stocking and sorting. By noticing patterns, asking questions, and showing compassion for a customer's time constraints, he created an experience that was personal and meaningful.

Both individuals excelled not because of their titles but because of their emotional awareness and intelligence. They understood that service is not just about action but about feeling.

Technology will forever continue to evolve; systems will grow sharper, data more predictive, and automation more sophisticated. But what cannot be replaced is the human-to-human bond. Intimacy and loyalty are born only through emotional engagement. Customers return not just for what is delivered, but for how they felt while receiving it.

When emotion is placed at the foundation of service, brands create relationships that last. But this intimacy is fragile: if emotions are ignored, bonds can snap, often permanently. This is why every person in the service chain, whether as an individual, a part of a team, or the essence of the business itself, must treat emotion not as a liability but as a strength. It must be cultivated, balanced, and expressed with awareness and intelligence.

Because in the end, service is not only about efficiency or outcomes. It is about trust, and trust is always emotional at its core.

Emotion at the Heart of Every Encounter

I still remember the incident as if it happened yesterday, though it was more than three decades ago. I was working at a petrol pump outlet with a branded car rental company in Mumbai. Starting out in my professional journey, I was young, energetic, proud of what I was doing, and eager to prove myself. It was a national holiday and hence, I had placed a small national flag to mark the day.

An elderly gentleman approached me with his grandson and asked about a self-drive car. I engaged with them enthusiastically, asking how long they planned to stay, whether they were tourists or locals, and suggesting options for their trip. While I was conversing with them, I noted that the young boy was staring intently at the flag. His grandfather noticed it too, and he curiously asked me, “You have a flag here; could you tell me its significance?”

For a moment, I froze. I wanted to give the right answer, but I wasn’t prepared. I wanted to be extra cautious about how I presented myself, and because of that, I ended up staying silent. In the meantime, the old man added, “Perhaps my grandson has learned about it in school.” Nodding away, the boy confidently explained the details. I felt a pang of embarrassment and I felt emotionally frazzled. That small experience made me wonder- How often do we just do something without really knowing why we are doing it?

That moment taught me an unforgettable lesson: emotional connection requires knowledge and authenticity. If I was going to place the flag on my desk, I had to understand its meaning, not just use it as a decoration or put it just because everyone else had. I immediately called a friend afterward to learn more, determined never to be caught unprepared again.

As I walked the old man and his grandson out, I told them, “I want to continue our discussion about the flag.” I explained what

I had learned, and the genuine smile of the gentleman told me that he was impressed by my effort to reflect and correct myself. With a smile, I gave them a spare flag that I had. That experience built a bond that has stayed in my memory for over 32 years.

What this incident reinforced for me is that EQ in service means recognizing when you are emotionally unprepared, correcting yourself, and engaging sincerely. Customers don't expect perfection, but they do expect honesty, humility, and respect.

There was also another memorable incident during my career that showed me the importance of being emotionally composed in any customer interaction.

I was a senior steward on a flight, serving the business class section. While I was serving meals, we had run out of a particular dessert option. The last passenger I reached was a foreign national seated next to an Indian passenger. Unfortunately, the Indian dessert he wanted was no longer available, as the last one of it had already been served to his neighbor.

The foreign gentleman was visibly upset. Despite my polite apologies and attempts to offer alternative continental desserts, he became increasingly agitated and very upset at me because he thought I was indifferent. His reaction was almost childlike; he was angry, insistent, and disappointed. In such moments, the instinctive and human reaction would be to lose patience or allow irritation to creep into the tone. But I knew that my role was to remain calm, collected, and professional.

I kept my emotions in check, listened without interruption, and reassured him that I would do everything possible to make up for the inconvenience. I presented all remaining dessert options, including another Indian sweet dish, and spoke to him with steady courtesy. Eventually, he agreed to try one of the alternatives. By the end of the meal, his demeanor softened, and he seemed content.

When I went to greet passengers at the end of the flight, the same gentleman surprised me by apologizing. He admitted he had been unnecessarily harsh over something as trivial as dessert. I simply smiled and said, "I understand, sir. My intention was never to be indifferent, and I truly wanted you to enjoy your meal." In that moment, the irritation he had felt transformed into mutual respect.

The lesson here was profound; that emotional intelligence in service is not about controlling the customer's emotions, but about controlling your own. By staying calm and respectful, irrespective of how the customer is presenting themselves, you create space for the situation to de-escalate. And sometimes, that restraint turns a negative interaction into a positive memory

Balancing Professionalism with Empathy

We have explored how and why emotions in service are a golden trait.

Yet this same trait, when left unrestrained and unchecked, can become a double-edged sword. Many service professionals, while trying their best to embody this necessary trait, fall into the trap of becoming overly emotional. They want to please everyone, avoid conflict at all costs, and sometimes go out of their way to connect, even if it disrupts the flow of service.

The intention here is good, but the outcome can be damaging. Processes may be delayed, standards compromised, or fairness sacrificed. The opposite is equally risky: when professionalism dominates and the human element is stripped away, customers leave feeling as if they've been served by a machine. The challenge, and the art, is to hold both in balance. Professionalism ensures consistency, fairness, and reliability, while empathy ensures warmth, connection, and trust. Together, they form the heartbeat of great service.

Emotional intelligence teaches us that empathy is not about giving in to every emotional pull. It is about acknowledging the customer's feelings while guiding them toward resolution within the framework of professionalism. This balance allows service to remain both human and effective.

Consider the scenario in a bank. A customer arrives visibly distressed about a loan approval, worried about whether it will come through in time. A professional who leans only on rules may say bluntly, "Applications take 10 working days. You'll get a message once processed." The customer leaves feeling dismissed, their anxiety unaddressed.

Now picture another officer who balances empathy with professionalism. They begin by acknowledging the emotion: "I can only imagine why you're anxious; this is an important matter." Then, they shift to professional clarity: "Here's what we can do: I'll help you ensure the form is complete so it doesn't face delays, and I'll flag it internally to check its progress. While the final approval will still follow standard timelines, you'll at least know where things stand."

This approach reassures the customer emotionally and builds a connect while keeping the process intact. The customer leaves not just with information, but with a sense of being cared for and respected—two things that drive trust far more than rules alone.

Contrast this with an episode in a healthcare establishment. A receptionist at a diagnostic lab meets a patient who is frightened of needles. Wanting to be compassionate, she spends a long time chatting, trying to soothe the fear, even suggesting they could reschedule if the patient isn't ready. Her empathy is genuine, but by delaying, she creates a backlog in the waiting room. Other patients, who are also anxious in their own way, now have to wait longer. The schedule is disrupted, staff become stressed, and efficiency collapses.

Here, empathy overshadowed professionalism. The right balance would have been to comfort the patient by saying, "It's normal to feel nervous, and our technician will make it quick and gentle," and guiding them toward the procedure promptly. This would have reassured the patient while still maintaining fairness and efficiency for everyone else.

From the customer's side, this balance is everything. They want to feel emotionally respected, but they also want their issue resolved. Too much empathy without action feels indulgent. Too much professionalism without warmth feels robotic. But when both come together, it builds confidence: "They understood me, and they also solved my problem-" Is the ultimate mindset that the customer wants to slip into. That is the emotional memory customers carry long after the interaction ends.

Balance is the true measure of emotional intelligence in service; it is not just about feeling more but about feeling right. It is the ability to read the room, adjust your tone, and manage your own emotions so that the customer feels cared for without service standards being compromised. Just like energy and enthusiasm need to be delicately balanced to prove effective, the same is true for emotions. Professionals who master this balance stand out because they do more than deliver service. They create trust. And in service, trust is the strongest currency of all

Emotional Agility in Moments that Matter

Pressure is a constant in service. Systems go down, lines get long, deliveries arrive late, and several people want different things at the same time. Emotional agility is the ability to stay steady, think clearly, and respond helpfully while the environment is noisy, fast, or uncertain. It does not mean suppressing emotion. It means guiding it well and using composure to create space for good decisions and using warmth to keep trust intact. Yet another moment that really matters is staying balanced when a customer is rude, overtly demanding, or seemingly unreasonable. In both situations, the professional's emotional steadiness becomes the customer's anchor.

In high-pressure service moments, three capabilities work together: presence, prioritization, and tone control.

Presence is the habit of arriving fully in the moment. The professional notices what matters now, not the last five problems or the next five tasks. A retail floor manager, for example, hears three requests at once—a price check, a spill, and a complaint about a fitting room. Instead of reacting in fragments, she makes eye contact with the nearest customer and says, "I'm with you," signals a colleague for the spill with a clear hand gesture, and radios the price check to inventory. That small sequence tells everyone: you are seen, and this is under control.

Prioritization is the calm sorting of what must happen first, second, and third. In a clinic reception during a morning rush, an administrator quietly triages: emergencies first, pre-booked patients next, walk-ins after. She communicates the order openly— "We'll take emergencies immediately, then scheduled patients; walk-ins, I'll keep you posted on the time window"—so expectations are set, frustration is reduced, and the queue feels fair.

Tone control is the craft of sounding composed even when the mind is working at speed. Think of a head chef during a dinner rush. Orders pile up, a fryer fails, and a supplier calls with a shortage. The chef's voice stays low and specific: "Table twelve, hold mains two minutes. Switch station three to pasta. Call maintenance to the fryer now." The kitchen mirrors that tone and the calmness guide the team forward.

Techniques That Help Under Pressure

While it is easy to theoretically understand the need of maintaining emotional composure in high-stakes moments, it is not always easy to practically implement. The same humanity that is a strength in most service situations may also become a weakness for service professionals, because they may end up reacting in a very spontaneous and instinctively emotional way.

Here are a few methods to help professionals navigate such moments while retaining their emotions and composure:

- **Breathe–Brief–Bridge.** One slow breath to reset; a brief, factual statement of what is happening; then a bridge to what you will do next. "We've had a system interruption. I'm moving your request to a manual queue now and will confirm your number before you go."
- **Name–Normalize–Navigate.** Name the emotion ("I can hear the worry in your voice"), normalize it ("anyone

in your situation would feel that"), then navigate to action ("here's the fastest route to a fix").

- **Choice architecture.** Offer two good options rather than one blunt answer. "We can rebook you on the next departure, or hold your fare and notify you the moment today's flight clears—what works better?"
- **Micro-updates.** In a long wait, silence is the enemy. A 90-second update every ten minutes keeps emotion from spiralling, even if the content hasn't changed much.

These tools are simple, but in pressure they separate scattered reactions from credible leadership.

Holding Steady with Difficult Customers

Not every customer arrives balanced. Some are rude or curt from fatigue, some are sharp from fear, and a few test boundaries. Emotional intelligence does not mean absorbing disrespect or rewarding unreasonable demands; it means responding without mirroring the unhelpful emotion, protecting fairness, and guiding the interaction back to purpose.

Service people often care deeply, and that's exactly why they sometimes get pulled off balance. They want to help and they want to be liked. When confronted with rudeness, two counterproductive reflexes can appear. One is appeasement; the professionals over-apologize, bend rules, or promise that which cannot be delivered, just to make the discomfort stop. The other is counter-emotion. They end up becoming defensive, curt, or sarcastic. Both erode trust and either create unfairness (to other customers or colleagues) or escalate conflict. The discipline is to hold a third path: firm empathy.

Consider this example: A traveller, delayed earlier in the day, marches to the counter and insists on a complimentary business-class upgrade "because I've suffered enough." The agent listens without interruption, acknowledges the day has been rough, and then sets a boundary with clarity and kindness: "I can see why you'd want the most comfortable option after the delay. Complimentary upgrades are not something I can authorize. What I can do now is move you to an aisle with extra legroom and pre-board you so you settle in sooner. Would you like me to do that?"

The customer hears no to the unreasonable demand and yes to a reasonable accommodation. The tone stays mature, the queue keeps moving, and fairness holds.

On the flip side is this instance, when a customer arrives angry at a bank about a charge. A reactive staffer might argue policy or match the volume. This will offer no resolution, and will instead agitate the customer even further. Instead, a balanced banker keeps voice low and steady, asks for one minute to pull the account history, and then explains the fee, the conditions under which it was applied, and the options to avoid it in future. If a one-time waiver is permissible, they offer it while emphasizing the learned prevention: "I've waived it today and set an alert so this doesn't catch you again." The customer feels treated as a person, not a rule; the bank preserves boundaries and respect.

Practical Checkpoints To Protect Professionalism

- **The tone ladder.** Start warm. If rudeness continues, keep language respectful while removing unnecessary apologies: move from "I'm so sorry" to "Here's what I can do" to "This is the policy I must follow." The message tightens while the respect remains.

- **One-breath rule.** Before replying to a provocation, take one breath. That second prevents the emotional echo that turns moments into battles.
- **Boundary phrases.** Prepare neutral lines that hold the line without shaming: "I want to help, and I can't do that while being spoken to like this. If we can keep the conversation respectful, I'll do everything within policy to resolve this."
- **Escalation with dignity.** When escalation is needed, frame it as added support, not punishment or a threat: "I'm bringing in my supervisor because they have more tools than I do in this situation."
- **Aftercare for the team.** Difficult interactions deplete energy. Short debriefs—"What worked? What will we do differently next time?"—turn stress into learning and protect morale.

When customers meet a professional who stays composed under pressure and firm with dignity when challenged, two things happen simultaneously. Emotionally, they feel contained—the situation has edges, someone is steering, the environment is safe. Practically, they get progress—clear next steps, realistic options, and follow-through. Even when the outcome is not exactly what they wanted, the memory tends to be positive because they were treated fairly and like an adult. That feeling the customer is left with, that "they understood me and they handled it well," is what keeps trust intact after hard moments.

Think of the emotionally agile professional as someone who sets the tone for everyone around them. It's like the difference between a thermometer and thermostat; the former only shows how hot or cold a room is but the latter decides the temperature and keeps the room steady.

In the same way, a good service professional doesn't just copy the customer's mood or get carried away by the chaos of the situation. If the customer is angry, they don't get angry back. If things are hectic, they don't add to the noise. Instead, they stay calm and steady, which helps everyone else feel calmer too. Their behavior quietly signals: "It's under control and we'll get this sorted."

Micro-Expressions of Emotion that Build Trust

Micro-expressions in service are not the fleeting facial cues psychologists often study in lie detection, but the small, deliberate signals of respect, warmth, and attentiveness that service professionals use to make a customer feel valued. They are tiny behaviors, so subtle that they can easily go unnoticed. But when they come together, they form the emotional texture of any interaction. Customers rarely remember the technical details of a service exchange, but they almost always remember how these micro-expressions made them feel.

The Categories of Micro-Expressions in Service

Facial cues

- A genuine smile that softens tension or welcomes the customer.

- Raised eyebrows of interest when a customer explains a concern, signaling attentiveness.
- A sympathetic expression with a slight head tilt, softened eyes, etc. that communicates understanding.

Vocal cues

- A patient pause before replying, which shows listening rather than rushing.
- Tone modulation; speaking with warmth and calmness rather than clipped efficiency.
- Using a customer's name naturally in the conversation to signal personal recognition.

Body language

- Leaning slightly forward when listening, showing genuine attention.
- Nodding gently while a customer speaks to acknowledge and affirm their input.
- Open posture with hands visible and arms uncrossed, to signal openness and availability.

Gestural habits

- Offering a small explanatory gesture, like pointing with the full hand instead of a finger.
- A slight bow of the head when handing something over, indicating respect.
- Subtle mirroring of the customer's rhythm, which creates unconscious rapport.

These micro-expressions are like punctuation in language. On their own, they are small, but they change the meaning and emotional tone of the "sentence" of service. A warm smile when saying, "Your table will be ready in two minutes," transforms a wait into a moment of reassurance. A flat face with the same words communicates irritation or indifference.

Teaching Micro-Expressions to Individuals

Training individuals starts with awareness. Many professionals don't realize how powerful these small gestures are, or how customers interpret them.

- **Roleplay and reflection**: Trainees can practice the same service phrase in multiple ways—monotone vs. warm, rushed vs. measured pause—and reflect on how it feels.
- **Mirror practice**: Staff can observe their own expressions in short exercises to become aware of their natural habits and refine them.
- **Feedback loops**: Colleagues or supervisors give feedback not just on the words used, but on micro-expressions: "Your smile didn't reach your eyes," or "That pause helped the customer feel heard."

For example, in a call center, trainers can record agents' tone when delivering scripted answers, then replay them to highlight how a slight upward inflection can turn a simple "I'll check that for you" into a genuine assurance, versus a robotic line.

Inculcating Micro-Expressions in Teams

As we saw earlier, 'We' is always more important than 'I' in service. The best of outcomes are possible only when everyone works towards a common goal. Hence, it is imperative that the whole team must also have the same emotional quotient. The team, as a unit, must align so that these micro-cues are consistent. A single empathetic cashier is good, but a consistently warm team across counters creates a brand identity.

- **Shared rituals**: Teams might start meetings by practicing greetings or tone exercises to set the day's emotional standard.
- **Shadowing**: New team members can shadow experienced staff not just for process, but to observe micro-expressions in live interactions.
- **Team agreements**: For example, in a hotel lobby, the rule might be: Every staff member acknowledges every guest they pass with a nod or greeting, whether or not they are directly serving them.

Embedding Micro-Expressions into Culture

At the cultural level, micro-expressions become the brand's invisible signature. Customers begin to expect them and associate them with the brand's personality.

- **Hiring**: Recruit for warmth, not just technical skill. A smile in an interview may say more than a résumé.
- **Recognition**: Celebrate stories where micro-expressions changed the outcome—like a guest review praising the doorman's respectful greeting.

- **Codification**: Just as processes are documented, emotional standards can be, too—simple guidelines like "Always pause to listen fully before responding," or "Always acknowledge waiting guests with eye contact."

Luxury airlines, for instance, have ingrained cultural habits. Flight attendants kneel at eye level when speaking to seated passengers rather than towering over them. This is not just politeness; it's a codified micro-expression of respect and intimacy, and over time it becomes synonymous with the brand itself.

Such micro-expressions may be fleeting, but their impact is lasting. When individuals are taught to use them consciously, when teams practice them consistently, and when organizations embed them into their DNA, service becomes more than a function. It becomes an emotional experience. Customers often forget the technicalities of a transaction, but they never forget how a smile, a pause, or a gesture of respect made them feel. These little things, multiplied a thousand times across interactions, are what build trust and loyalty that no competitor can easily break.

Conclusion: The Lasting Currency of Emotion

In the evolving world of service, where technology races ahead with automation, instant updates, and flawless data, one thing remains unchanged: service without emotion is hollow. Customers may appreciate efficiency, but what they truly remember and what ultimately shapes their loyalty, is how a brand emotionally resonates or connects with them.

Emotions are the invisible currency of service. A smile at the right moment, a pause that conveys patience, a tone that softens a tense situation—these are not trivial details. They are the foundation of trust. When managed with intelligence, emotions become a strength that distinguishes great service from the merely functional. They create bonds that feel personal, intimate, and enduring.

But this currency is fragile. The absence of emotion in even the slightest way —can shatter relationships instantly. Brands at the top often stumble not because their products fail, but because the emotional thread with customers snaps, and once broken, it is rarely restored.

To treat emotion as a strength is to accept its dual nature: it must be present, but also balanced. Professionals must show care without indulgence, empathy without abandoning fairness, composure without coldness. This is what emotional intelligence truly means. It is the ability to hold one's own emotions steady while understanding and adapting to the emotions of others.

The doorman who greets like a host, the steward who diffuses anger with calm dignity, the cashier who slows down for a struggling parent—all of them prove that service excellence lives in small, human gestures. And when organizations nurture this at every level, including for the individual, team, and overall culture, they transform emotion from a risk into their greatest competitive advantage.

Because in the end, processes can be copied, products can be replicated, and technology can be bought. But the emotional experience of being treated with dignity, respect, and care is unique, special, and it is what customers return for again and again.

Verses Kindler Publication

Reach us through our website -

https://www.verseskindlerpublication.com/

For more information visit our

Instagram or Facebook page.